Introduction

The USAF's front line fighters during the Korean War were the F-86 Sabre, F-84 Thunderjet, P-82 Twin Mustang and F-80 Shooting Star – yet all but the F-86 were eclipsed when Soviet MiG-15s appeared over the battlefield.

Even as the conflict on the Korean peninsula died down, the danger of the ongoing cold war turning into a hot war continued to grow and the USAF understood that bold new fighter designs would be needed if it was to remain the most powerful air force in the world. Meanwhile, American designers had developed a better understanding of aerodynamics, new and more powerful engine designs were in the works and aviation technology was advancing in leaps and bounds. An entirely new generation of fighters was about to be born, all of which would be given three-digit designations: the Century Series fighters.

Although most were designed with a single purpose in mind, and prioritising speed and payload over stealth and manoeuvrability, as time passed the Century Series fighters would evolve to fulfil a wealth of different roles, some never even considered when they were designed.

Furthermore, technology continued to advance and evolve – as did the perceived threat from the East. Missile capability took priority over cannon; drop tanks and in-flight refuelling probes came to be more important than blistering acceleration; and fire control systems added new abilities at the expense of complexity and cost.

The Century Series fighters became an important stepping stone in postwar military aircraft design – spanning the period between the simple short-living designs of the late 1940s/early 1950s and the incredibly durable 'legacy' designs of the 1970s.

The central unifying characteristic of the Century Series fighters was the ability to fly faster than the speed of sound in level flight. Other than that, the aircraft can be divided into two groups: The fighter-bombers (F-100, F-101A and F-105) and the interceptors (F-101B, F-102, F-104, F-106). During the first flight of the first of the Century Series fighter, the F-100 Super Sabre, it was already evident that fighter design had entered a new era. The F-100 prototype broke the sound barrier straight away and many of the subsequent century series fighters went on to set both speed and altitude records.

It was, however, in front line service the Century Series fighters made a name for themselves – even if the type of warfare they encountered was very different from the theoretical combat scenarios they had been designed for. The F-100 became the close air support aircraft of choice in the Vietnam War. The F-101 Voodoo, originally designed as a long-range bomber escort, ended as both an interceptor and a photo reconnaissance aircraft. The F-105 Thunderchief began as a nuclear penetration fighter-bomber but ended up as a conventional bomber and a Wild Weasel aircraft. The F-104 became a frontline fighter in many of the world's air forces, where it assumed roles ranging from interceptor to ground attack aircraft. The two 'Deadly Deltas', the F-102 and F-106, remained Interceptors throughout their service. Arguably, the F-106 was the finest interceptor ever conceived.

The Century Series fighters had their heyday in the 1960s and 1970s, with the Vietnam War demonstrating that multirole aircraft were the future of military aircraft design. The aircraft that would replace the Century Series fighters were the Teen Series fighters, which would become the mainstay of the USAF as well as many other air forces around the world. These aircraft – the F-14, F-15, F-16 and F-18 – were being developed as technological advancement was entering a slower phase of maturity. The limits of what could be readily achieved had been reached and refinement with reliability was the name of the game.

Yet Teen Series fighters would never have been possible without the valuable lessons learned from the mighty Century Series fighters and their remarkable history in both development and in combat.

ABOUT MADS BANGSØ

For as long as I can remember I've been drawing aircraft, the goal has always been to create illustrations that were as authentic and as realistic as possible. Over the years I've been experimenting with a wide variety of different media ranging from colour pencils to airbrushes. I've settled on 3D computer graphics, and take great pride in creating each aircraft profile from the ground up.

My main focus when illustrating an aircraft is not only to represent its colours and markings, but also to tell its story in peeling paint, wear and tear, bleached patches, reflections, dirt and grime. My hope is that a front line USAF F-100 with many CAS missions under its belt looks very different from a well-maintained Belgian F-104 despite both being painted using the same colours. The same goes for the drone aircraft which show signs of severe neglect when compared to the sleek and clean aircraft that were used in the ADC squadrons.

Working on this Century Series Fighters book proved a great challenge, but also immensely rewarding knowing that this book may remind you, the reader, of these amazing looking aircraft and the people who maintained and flew them.

This book is dedicated to Ib Kyhl

Thanks:
Scott Brown, Wit Raymond, Rock Roszak, The Scanmasters, Steven O´Hara and Dan Sharp

CONTENTS

All illustrations:
MADS BANGSØ

Design:
BURDA

Publisher:
STEVE O'HARA

Editor:
DAN SHARP

Published by:
**MORTONS MEDIA GROUP LTD,
MEDIA CENTRE,
MORTON WAY,
HORNCASTLE,
LINCOLNSHIRE
LN9 6JR.**

Tel. **01507 529529**

Printed by:
**WILLIAM GIBBONS
AND SONS,
WOLVERHAMPTON**

MORTONS
MEDIA GROUP LTD

ISBN: 978-1-911639-70-1

NORTH AMERICAN F-100 SUPER SABRE

1953 1979

Combat experience during the Korean War had demonstrated the need for advanced aircraft able to provide both supersonic performance and fighter-bomber capability. North American's response was the F-100 – the first Century Series fighter.

Even as the F-86 Sabre was entering service with the USAF, North American designers Raymond Rice and Edgar Schmued were already considering developments that would significantly improve its performance. Initially, their attention was focused on the F-86's wings and tailplane – increasing the sweepback from 35° to 45° and relocating the tailplane lower down. The company was confident enough in this 'Sabre 45' project, begun in February 1949, to fund the modification of an XF-86D with these features.

An 'Advanced F-86D' proposal was eventually submitted to the USAF in August 1950, two months after the

beginning of the Korean War. Although the Air Force was not able to take it forward at that time, North American was given a strong indication that the proposal would eventually be accepted. Work therefore continued on an 'Advanced F-86E', with the design receiving the internal designation NA-180.

After two years of development, the NA-180 had little in common with the original F-86. It was larger and heavier with a host of novel features and was propelled by a much more powerful engine than its predecessor. North American had intended to equip the NA-180 with radar to make it a useful interceptor capable of replacing the F-86D but the USAF

simply wanted was a straightforward high-performance day fighter armed with a quartet of 20mm cannon.

Following a full-scale mock-up inspection on November 9, 1951, requests were made for more than 100 separate changes to the design. The cockpit canopy was extended, the tailplanes were moved lower down and the shape of the fuselage was altered. Nevertheless, and despite concerns that the type would be too complicated, the USAF commissioned two prototypes and 110 full production fighter aircraft based on what was now the NA-192 design. The official designation 'F-100' was allocated the following month.

F-100A-5-NA SUPER SABRE (54-5775) ▽

ADRC Air Development and Research Center, 1954. This aircraft was among the first Super Sabres produced – a 'short-tail' A model. This aircraft would later become part of the New Mexico ANG and was damaged beyond repair after suffering a hard landing on October 9, 1962. The pilot, 2/Lt David R McCauley, suffered severe burns but survived the crash.

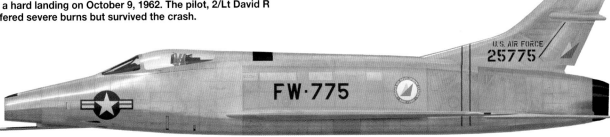

▽ F-100C-5-NA SUPER SABRE (53-1774)

322nd Fighter Day Group, 451sf Fighter Day Squadron, 1956. Notice the placement of the stars-and-bars insignia on this aircraft. National insignia would be carried on the nose early on in the F-100's career, but from 1957 onward it was moved to the rear fuselage. This aircraft was sent to MASDC on January 17, 1972, but would later become part of the Turkish AF.

▽ F-100C-25-NA SUPER SABRE (54-2101)

479th Fighter Day Group, 434th Fighter Day Squadron 'Red Devils', 1957. This aircraft is adorned with multi-coloured fuselage bands indicating that this aircraft was assigned to the wing commander.

North American F-100 Super Sabre

Work on the first YF-100A commenced at the company's facility in Inglewood, Los Angeles, in early 1952 and further changes to the design were made on the run. The nose was made 9in longer, the tailplanes and fin were reduced in length but given greater chord and, in order to save weight, self-sealing fuel tanks were replaced with non-self-sealing tanks.

The USAF requested drop tank capability for increased range in October 1952 – necessitating the design of a new stronger wing – and developing

this resulted in further delays. The initial YF-100A prototype, serial 52-5754, was completed on April 24, 1953. It was powered by a single Pratt & Whitney XJ57-P-7 non-afterburning turbojet (the series production model would have an afterburner) providing 8500lb-ft of thrust. The aircraft was then transported to Edwards Air Force Base in preparation for flight testing.

Its first flight, with Second World War ace turned North American test pilot George S 'Wheaties' Welch at the

controls, took place on May 25, 1953. Despite the lack of an afterburner, Welch managed to break the sound barrier in level flight at 30,000ft during the 55-minute flight. He did it again during a second flight 20 minutes later on the same day. The aircraft could go supersonic with ease above 30,000ft and could even approach the sound barrier at low level.

The same aircraft hit Mach 1.44 on July 6, 1953, during a dive from 51,000ft, and shortly thereafter the USAF

F-100C-20-NA SUPER SABRE (54-1878) ▽

36th Tactical Fighter Wing, 32nd Tactical Fighter Squadron (USAFE) 'Wolfhounds', late 1958. The squadron was operating out of Soesterberg AB in Holland. 54-1878 would be sent to the Military Aircraft Storage and Disposition Center (MASDC) on March 14, 1974, but later become a part of the Turkish AF. The aircraft would remain in service until well into the 80s.

F-100D-65-NA SUPER SABRE (56-3000) ▽

20th Tactical Fighter Wing, 1958. The CO aircraft of the 20th Tactical Fighter Wing is among the most well-known F-100s ever to fly. The aircraft, known as 'Triple Zilch', is sporting the trim colours of the squadrons that comprised the wing: the 55th, 77th and 79th Tactical Fighter Squadrons, as well as the squadron patches. The aircraft sported this paint scheme in the late 50s while the wing was operating out of RAF Wethersfield and RAF Woodbridge. 56-3000 is today on display at the home base of the Texas ANG: Lackland AFB. However, it wears the colours of the Texas ANG rather than those of Triple Zilch.

requested fighter-bomber capability for the F-100, prompting North American to add bomb rack attachment points to the new drop-tank capable wing design it was already working on.

The second prototype, serial 52-5755, flew for the first time on October 14, 1953, with Welch again at the controls. Five days later an event was arranged to showcase the aircraft for the press. Welch stunned the assembled journalists by making a high-speed pass just feet from the ground which reportedly shattered the windows of the Palmdale airport administration building.

A week later the first production model F-100A, serial 52-5756, made its flight debut. Another Second World War veteran, Colonel Frank Kendall 'Pete' Everest, set a new world air speed record of 755.149mph in the aircraft that same day – breaking the previous record of 752.9mph set 26 days earlier by the US Navy's James B Verdin flying a Douglas F4D Skyray.

North American triumphantly declared that it had constructed the world's first operational supersonic fighter, but the design still had numerous flaws which needed to be addressed. Poor visibility over the nose made take-offs and landings difficult, it was a handful at low speeds, longitudinal stability was lacking at high speeds and climb rate was far less than desired. Rudder flutter was also a problem early on but this was corrected with the aid of hydraulic dampers.

The first operational unit to receive the F-100A was the 479th Fighter Day Wing of Tactical Air Command, based at George Air Force Base. Deliveries commenced in late November 1953 and North American made further changes to the design even as aircraft were rolling off the production line. The 104th F-100A received cockpit modifications and from the 168th example the F-100A was powered by the Pratt & Whitney J57-P-39 with 16,000lb-ft of thrust. The last of 203 examples was constructed in April 1955.

F-100F-1-NA SUPER SABRE (56-3730) ▽

20th Tactical Fighter Wing, 55th Tactical Fighter Squadron 'Fighting Fifty Fifth', 1960. This aircraft served with a multitude of units before it was sent to MASDC on September 14, 1977. Since 2006 it has been on display at the USAF Academy, Colorado Springs, Colorado.

F-100D-90-NA SUPER SABRE (56-3262) ▽

48th Tactical Fighter Squadron, 492nd Tactical Fighter Squadron 'Bolars', 1959. Prior to the Vietnam war, the USAF was not shy about adding a bit of colour to its aircraft. The 48th TFW applied some particular flashy paint schemes to its aircraft when participating in a weapons meet at Nellis AFB in 1959. The 492nd, 493rd and 494th FTS all had at least one aircraft painted like this in the squadron's respective trim colours (blue, yellow and red) and the CO aircraft that sported all three colours. Even for this era it was a very colourful aircraft.

F-100D-90-NA SUPER SABRE (56-3264) ▽

405th Tactical Fighter Wing, 510th Tactical Fighter Squadron 'Buzzards', 1961. 56-3264 was part of a detachment deployed at Thailand's Don Muang Airport in the spring of 1961. The aircraft would remain in SEA throughout the 60s with the 405th. On August 22, 1967, the aircraft was hit by AAA fire. The pilot managed to fly the crippled F-100 out over the South China Sea and eject, before being rescued by a US Army helicopter.

North American F-100 Super Sabre

42009

US AIR F

F-100D-20-NA (55-3520) ▼

USAF Demonstration team Thunderbirds, 1967. The F-100 was unique in serving with the Thunderbirds, being retired, and then being reinstated to the Thunderbirds inventory once again. In 1956 the Thunderbirds received F-100Cs which they operated until 1964, when they were replaced with the F-105B Thunderchief. The huge aircraft proved unsuitable for the role and the Thunderbirds decided to revert to the F-100 in July 1964, only this time they received F-100Ds. 55-3520 flew as the solo aircraft. The aircraft crashed on October 21, 1967 at Laughlin AFB, TX, after the engine exploded during a high g pull-up. The pilot did manage to bail out and survived the incident.

U.S. AI

These early F-100s were generally disliked by their pilots – with the difficulty of flying the aircraft at low speeds resulting in a high accident rate. At around this time, six F-100As had their cannon replaced with a set of five cameras beneath the cockpit to become RF-100As and were usually operated with four drop tanks instead of the usual F-100A load of two.

Back in December 1953, the USAF had decided that the last 70 F-100As off the production line should be modified as fighter-bombers with the new drop-tank and bomb-carrying wing – this was North American's NA-214 design, later to be redesignated F-100Cs. Consequently,

on February 24, 1954, an order was placed for 230 F-100Cs, increasing to 564 by May 27.

North American converted the fourth F-100A off the line into the YF-100C prototype and each wingtip was extended 12in (this 2ft wingspan increase later being added to the regular F-100A production line). The wings themselves were adapted to carry drop tanks or up to 5000lb of external stores. The F-100C also had a removable in-flight refuelling probe installed under its starboard wing. The earliest examples of this were straight but the design was later changed to incorporate an upwards curve, which made it easier for the pilot to see it when

they were attempting to mate the probe with the drogue.

On September 27, 1954, the USAF ordered that many of the pre-ordered F-100Cs should be built as F-100Ds instead, while two days later the 479th finally became operational with the F-100A. The F-100D was to feature another new wing design – now with greater chord at the wingroot, increasing overall wing area and thereby decreasing landing speed. Explosive bolts allowed the underwing pylons to be jettisoned and a centreline hardpoint was added, along with electronic countermeasures, an AN/APS-54 tail warning radar and an AN/AJB-1 low-altitude bombing system.

▼ F-100C-25-NA SUPER SABRE (54-2009)

USAFE Demonstration Team 'Skyblazers', 1957. This aircraft is currently on display at Luke AFB in Arizona.

The F-100D also added support for the Sidewinder heat-seeking air-to-air missile.

One severe defect of the F-100A had not yet been detected by this point, however, and was therefore still part of the F-100D's design: the fin. Its diminutive size caused directional instability and it had not yet been realised that extreme manoeuvring would put it under a dangerous amount of strain – which only increased when drop tanks were fitted.

The ninth production model F-100A, serial 52-5764, broke up during a test dive and recovery on October 12, 1954, killing Welch. Experienced flyer Geoffrey Stephenson of the British Central Fighter

Establishment, was then killed in similar circumstances while evaluating an F-100A. Another US pilot, Major Frank N Emory, barely managed to escape when a third F-100A came apart during a high-g manoeuvre.

This was the final straw – all of the remaining 180 F-100As (68 in service, 112 complete but undelivered) being grounded pending an urgent investigation. Attention was quickly focused on the fin and a new version with 27% more vertical area was hastily designed. The first full production model F-100C was completed on October 19, 1954, and conditionally accepted ten days later even though the flight ban remained in place.

The bigger fin was incorporated into the F-100A assembly line early in 1955 – the 184th example being built with it – and all existing F-100As had it retrofitted. The problem was cured and the flight ban was lifted, allowing test pilot Al White to take the first F-100C up for its first flight on January 17, 1955, nearly three months after it was built (even though it still had the small fin fitted). F-100C deliveries to the 450th Fighter Day Squadron commenced in April.

The last F-100As were delivered in July 1955, just as the 450th were becoming operational, and Colonel Harold Hanes set a new world air-speed record with the first F-100C on August 20 at 822.135mph.

North American F-100 Super Sabre

0-53604

F-100D-50-NA SUPER SABRE (55-2894) ▽

3rd Tactical Fighter Wing, 416th Tactical Fighter Squadron 'Silver Knights', 1965. Although the F-100 flew many MIGCAP missions in Vietnam there is no official record of an F-100 aerial victory. However, there are indications that an F-100 shot down a MiG-17 on April 4, 1965. Captain Donald Kilgus was flying 55-2894 as escort for a flight of 48 F-105Ds when four MIG-17s came into sight. Kilgus dived from 20,000ft and fired his four 20mm guns at one of the MiGs. Kilgus saw debris falling away from the MIG and a bright flash from the tail. The MiG descended through a haze and Kilgus lost sight of it. Several pilots reported that they saw the MiG hit the ground, but the kill was never confirmed.

U.S. AIR FORCE

F-100D-25-NA SUPER SABRE (55-3602) ▽

27th Tactical Fighter Wing, 481st Tactical Fighter Squadron 'Crusaders', 1965. The 27th TFW deployed individual squadrons to Tan Son Nhut AB in Vietnam, rather than the entire wing being deployed to a single base. 55-3602 would later be transferred to the 308th TFS and eventually lost on September 24, 1968, while conducting a mission over South Vietnam. The pilot was killed.

U.S. AIR FORCE

F-100D-25-NA SUPER SABRE (55-3604)

3rd Tactical Fighter Wing, 416th Tactical Fighter Squadron 'Silver Knights', 1965. Early in the Vietnam war, the 3rd TFW was stationed at Bien Hoa AB. 55-3206 made it through the war and would eventually be sent to MASDC on June 9, 1978, only to later be revived as a QF-100D drone.

North American F-100 Super Sabre

Four months later, North American was contracted to build a two-seat trainer prototype, the TF-100C. This was essentially a standard F-100C with a yard-long fuselage extension added to allow the accommodation of the second seat.

The F-100D had meanwhile supplanted the F-100C on the production line and the first example made its flying debut on January 24, 1956. The F-100C was adopted by the USAF's Thunderbirds display team commencing on May 19,

1956, and the first TF-100C flew for the first time on August 3. The latter crashed during a spinning test but it was deemed a success nonetheless and a production order followed for the type, now redesignated as the F-100F.

Deliveries of the F-100D to the 405th Fighter-Bomber Wing at Langley Air Force Base commenced in September 1956. These were plagued by engine issues, unreliable bomb release systems, inaccurate fire control systems and

electrical problems – but upgrades and updates gradually turned the F-100D into a fully serviceable machine.

The first F-100F took to the air on March 7, 1957, piloted by George Mace, with deliveries beginning in January 1958. It had a single-piece canopy which covered both seats but otherwise retained most of the F-100D's features.

The last F-100 rolled off the production line in October 1959 for a grand total of 2294 built (two YF-100As, 203 F-100As,

451 F-100Cs, 940 F-100Ds and 339 F-100Fs). The aircraft served extensively with the USAF in Vietnam – primarily in the ground-attack role – and the last operational F-100 mission was flown by the Air National Guard on November 10, 1979.

FOREIGN SERVICE AND COMBAT
Four foreign air forces operated the F-100 – the Republic of China, aka Taiwan, France, Denmark and Turkey. The ROCAF received 80 refurbished and upgraded F-100As, six F-100Fs and four RF-100As between October 1958 and 1960. These were eventually followed, in the early 1970s, by a further 38 F-100As and

eight F-100Fs. The type was retired from Taiwanese service during the early 1980s.

Under the US Mutual Defense Assistance Program (MAP), France received 85 new F-100Ds and 15 new F-100Fs, with deliveries commencing in 1958. These served throughout the 1960s before being withdrawn in the mid-1970s. Starting a year later than France but under the same programme, Denmark received 48 new F-100Ds and 10 new F-100Fs. These were then upgraded to include Martin-Baker ejection seats, Saab-built bomb sights and a rolling map display. Although the first batch of Danish F-100s were retired in the early 1970s, in

1974 the Danes received an additional 14 ex-USAF F-100Fs.

Turkey received the largest number of F-100s under MAP – 131 new F-100Ds and 50 F-100Fs. And a further 92 F-100Cs, former USAF aircraft, were delivered from 1972. The last airworthy Turkish F-100s were retired in 1988.

The USAF's Super Sabres first saw operational use during the summer of 1958 when American forces were sent to Beirut. F-100Ds flew top cover during the invasion but were not required to engage in combat. Four years later, F-100Ds were sent to Takhi Air Base in Thailand as American activities in Vietnam grew in

▼ F-100F-20-NA SUPER SABRE (58-1213)

35th Tactical Fighter Wing, 352nd Tactical Fighter Squadron 'Yellow Jackets', 1970. This aircraft operated out of Tuy Hoa AB, flying the famous Misty FAC missions. The goal of these missions was to disrupt supply route on the Ho Chi Minh Trail. The Misty FACs would fire marking rockets at targets of interest (SAM sites, AAA sites, bridges, trucks, boats etc.). These missions were extremely dangerous and 28% of all Misty FAC aircraft were shot down. 58-1213 survived only to be sent to MASDC on November 29, 1971.

▼ F-100D-90-NA SUPER SABRE (56-3287)

31st Tactical Fighter Wing, 308th Tactical Fighter Squadron 'Emerald Knights', 1969. The 31st TFW operated out of Tuy Hoa AB while deployed in Vietnam. 56-3287 was lost on a CAS mission over South Vietnam on June 30, 1970. The pilot managed to bail out and survived the crash.

North American F-100 Super Sabre

F-100D-20-NA SUPER SABRE (55-3508) ▽

35th Tactical Fighter Wing, 615th Tactical Fighter Squadron 'Screaming Eagles', 1971. The 615th TFS operated out of Phan Rhang AB in 1971. The 35th TFW was the last unit to operate the F-100 in Vietnam and on July 31, 1971, the wing withdrew and headed back to CONUS. This aircraft was one of the last F-100s to fly combat missions over Vietnam and would return to ANG duty back home. It eventually went to MASDC on January 12, 1978. Later it was converted to QF-100D standard.

F-100C-1-NA SUPER SABRE (54-1746) ▽

140th Tactical Fighter Group, 120th Tactical Fighter Squadron, Colorado Air National Guard, 1961. While most frontline squadrons were being equipped with the latest version of the Super Sabre, the ANG units would hang on to the C-models for a little while longer. This early Block 1 F-100C would join the Turkish AF on August 28, 1972.

▼ F-100F-20-NA SUPER SABRE (58-1221)

6234th Tactical Fighter Wing (provisional), Weasel Det., 1965. The Wild Weasel units were established to counter the growing threat of surface-to-air missiles (SAMs) facing US aircraft in Vietnam. The first attempt to counter the threat became known as Wild Weasel and involved specially modified two-seater F-100Fs carrying the AGM-45 Shrike anti-radiation missile, able to home in on the radars of SAM sites. Those missions were very dangerous and pilots would do just about anything to avoid the SAM sites, giving rise to the Wild Weasel motto: 'You Gotta Be Shittin' me' which apparently was the pilot's initial reaction when told the mission objective. 58-1221 was lost on March 13, 1966, due to engine failure during a training exercise.

North American F-100 Super Sabre

F-100D-45-NA SUPER SABRE (55-2181) ▼

149th Tactical Fighter Group, 182nd Tactical Fighter Squadron, Texas Air National Guard, 1974. This aircraft participated in the Red Flag exercise at Nellis AFB in 1974. TX ANG was among the last units to operate the F-100. It wasn't until 1979 that its remaining F-100s were transferred to MASDC. This aircraft ended its life as a QF-100D drone.

scale and scope. As the conflict escalated, F-100Ds were redeployed from Clark AFB in the Philippines to Da Nang AFB in South Vietnam. Their first combat mission, in secret, took place on June 9, 1964, with strikes against anti-aircraft sites in Laos. Operations became public knowledge that December and strikes against North Vietnam commenced in February 1965.

Forty F-100Ds and F-100Fs took part in Rolling Thunder attacks against the North on March 2, 1965, but thereafter the F-100 was used primarily for battlefield support in South Vietnam. The exception to this was the modification of four F-100Fs as 'Wild Weasel' EF-100Fs – equipping them with the electronics necessary to seek out enemy air defence systems. To begin with, the EF-100s were used to direct strike packages of F-105s onto the SAM sites but from 1966 three more EF-100F conversions were made and this time the aircraft were fitted with AGM-45 Shrike anti-radar missiles. This enabled them to not only seek out but also attack the enemy radar positions.

The EF-100Fs were soon replaced with more capable F-105Fs but the F-100 continued as the ubiquitous USAF fighter-bomber in Vietnam. A total of 198 were in-theatre at the beginning of 1967 and four more Air National Guard (ANG) Super Sabre squadrons joined the fray in 1968. The F-100 could deliver 750lb bombs, 2.75in rockets, napalm and cluster bombs as well as using its cannon for strafing. It quickly developed a reputation for arriving where it was needed quickly and returning quickly after reloading.

▼ F-100D-60-NA SUPER SABRE (56-2947)

103rd Tactical Fighter Group, 118th Tactical Fighter Squadron, Cincinnati Air National Guard, 1976. ANG units would continue to fly the F-100D and F models throughout the 70s. 56-2947 was a veteran of Project ZEL (ZEro-Length launch programme) where F-100s were fitted with a rocket powerful enough to launch them without the use of a runway. Later in its career this aircraft was converted into a QF-100D drone.

A number of F-100Fs were used as forward air controllers or FACs with the callsign 'Misty'. The aircraft would be flown into high-threat environments and the back-seater would be tasked with spotting targets before marking them with smoke rockets. This was an extremely risky mission and a total of seven F-100 'Misty' pilots were killed with another four being taken prisoner.

After some 360,000 sorties, the F-100 was finally retired from Vietnam in July 1971. By this point 186 of them had been shot down by AAA, another seven had been destroyed by enemy ground forces and 45 had been written off in accidents. Officially, no F-100 shot down an enemy aircraft and no F-100 was shot down by an enemy aircraft – despite Captain Donald Kilgus claiming a MiG-17 on April 4, 1965 (this being credited as a 'probable' rather than a 'kill'). ANG units continued to use the F-100 up to 1980 and the following year 325 F-100Ds and F-100Fs were converted to QF-100 drone configuration. These were fitted with chaff and flare dispensers as well as propane heaters in the wingtips which would help to attract Sidewinder missiles during target practice – keeping the missiles away from the engine and fuselage to increase survivability for future exercises.

The drones continued to be used into the 1990s and five were used by a civilian contractor before being retired in 2001.

North American F-100 Super Sabre

F-100A-10-NA SUPER SABRE (53-1540) ▽

23rd Fighter Squadron, Republic of China Air Force, 1971. No fewer than 118 F-100As would be delivered to the ROCAF. In order for them to fire the AIM-9 Sidewinder missile, a vertical stabilizer similar to that of the F-100D was retrofitted to the A-model aircraft. In this profile view the most distinguishable difference between this and a D-model is probably the lack of wing fences.

F-100D-10-NA SUPER SABRE (54-2219) ▽

171. Filo, Turkish Air Force, 1964. No fewer than 206 F-100s were operated by the Turkish Air Force, most supplied by the USAF but 23 coming from the RDAF when the aircraft was phased out of Danish service. The Turkish Air Force is the only other air force apart from the USAF to fly the F-100 in combat – when F-100s of the Turkish Air Force flew missions over Cyprus in 1974. 54-2219 was delivered to the Turkish AF on May 24, 1959, becoming one of the first F-100s to enter Turkish service.

F-100D-35-NA SUPER SABRE (55-2739) ▽

Escadron de Chasse 4/11 'Jura', Armée de l´Air, 1978. The French Air Force, Armée de l´Air, operated a total of 100 Super Sabres from 1958 to 1978. The last unit to operate the Super Sabre was Escadron de Chasse 4/11 'Jura', which was based in Djibouti in 1978. Those F-100s were adorned with a huge shark mouth – a unique feature for this unit. 55-2739 is preserved today at the Danish National Aircraft Museum and painted in the colours of an esk. 727 aircraft with the buzz number G-183.

31540

0105

42219

W-219

52739

North American F-100 Super Sabre

F-100D-10-NA SUPER SABRE (54-2177) ▼

Eskadrille 730, Royal Danish Air Force, 1977. During the latter half of the F-100's time in service with the RDAF, the aircraft were painted in dark green. The green colour proved very prone to weathering, causing some areas to get bleached while others remained glossy and more saturated. This finish served as a unique camouflage scheme until the F-100s were retired from RDAF service. 54-2177 would remain in service but with the Turkish AF – where it arrived on May 18, 1981. It was eventually scrapped in 1992.

F-100D-15-NA SUPER SABRE (54-2222)

Eskadrille 727, Royal Danish Air Force, 1969. 54-2222 was among 72 Super Sabres delivered to the RDAF on June 16, 1959. As the F-100s were being phased out of RDAF service in 1982, this aircraft was delivered to Turkey on January 26, 1982, and served with the Turkish AF until 1987.

QF-100F-15-NA SUPER SABRE (56-3904)

6585th Test Group, 1978. Two hundred and nine F-100Ds and Fs were converted into QF-100 drones operating out if Tyndall AFB, FL. These aircraft were flown with remote controls and were subject to missile testing and pilot training. Needless to say, most of these planes never served with another unit thereafter. 56-3904, however, never got through the conversion process and survives today. It was last noted as undergoing restoration at Eureka Spring, AR.

MCDONNELL F-101 VOODOO

1954-1982

Designed as one of the USAF's first supersonic fighters, McDonnell's F-101 Voodoo was the product of a troubled development programme and would end up being best known as a reconnaissance platform.

The first generation jet fighters designed during the Second World War all suffered from a particular handicap – lack of range. Early jet engines were incredibly thirsty and underpowered, which meant the quantity of fuel that could be carried was severely limited.

Therefore, at the beginning of 1946, the USAAF issued a requirement for a 'penetration' jet fighter that would have the range necessary to escort nuclear bombers to their targets and back. The specification was challenging but three companies submitted proposals which appeared sufficiently promising for the USAAF to commission prototypes: North American's YP-93A, Lockheed's XP-90 and McDonnell's XP-88. The latter was based on the firm's Model 36, designed by a team led by Edward M 'Bud' Flesh, and two examples were ordered on June 20, 1946.

Featuring low-set 35-degree sweptback wings, a conventional tail and wingroot intakes to feed a pair of Westinghouse J34-WE-13 turbojets with 3000lb-ft of thrust each built into its capacious fuselage, the XP-88 looked clean and purposeful – if rather large. It would be armed with six 20mm cannon. When the USAAF became the USAF, the XP-88s became XF-88s, and in keeping with company policy McDonnell gave the type a 'spook' name – Voodoo.

Assembly of the first example was completed on August 11, 1948, and it was first flown on October 20 that year, by company test pilot Robert M

F-101A-5-MC VOODOO (53-2426) ▽

1957. This one-of-a-kind version of the Voodoo was designated JF-101A after being fitted with upgraded Pratt & Whitney J57-P-55 engines. The J75-P-55s were noticeably longer than the F-101A's factory-fitted J57-P-13s. With the more powerful engines, this aircraft set a new speed record on December 12, 1957; Major Adrian Drew averaged 1207.6mph over a 10-mile stretch. The aircraft was send to the 309th Aerospace Maintenance and Regeneration Center (AMARC) in February 1961 but today is on static display at Cannon AFB, New Mexico.

▽ F-101A-25-MC VOODOO (54-1444)

81st Tactical Fighter Wing, 1962. The 81th TFW served as a nuclear deterrent force and operated out of RAF Bentwaters in the UK.

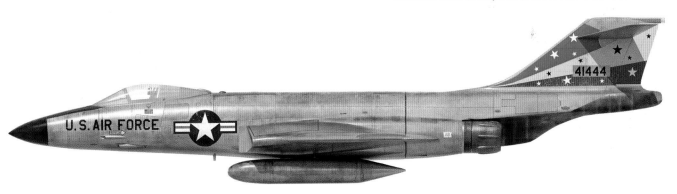

F-101B-95-MC VOODOO (57-0376) ▽

4735th Air Defense Group, 60th Fighter-Interceptor Squadron, 1959. The 60th FIS was the first unit to receive the Voodoo's F-101B variant. The first delivery took place on January 5, 1959. This aircraft had a relatively short career, being written off on November 14, 1967, after a collision with F-101B serial 57-0378.

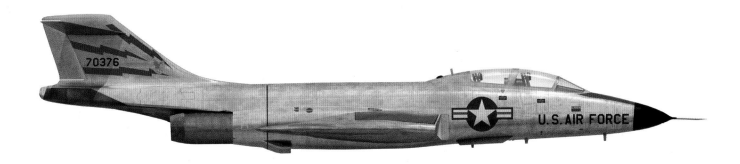

Mcdonnell F-101 Voodoo

Eldholm. It was immediately apparent that Westinghouse's engines were going to cause problems. While the aircraft's handling and endurance were as expected, it was unable to go supersonic with a top speed of just 641mph. Consequently, the second XF-88 was retrofitted with afterburners of McDonnell's own design, turning the J34-WE-13s into J34-WE-22s which could provide 3600lb-ft thrust each.

The resulting XF-88A first flew on April 26, 1949, and performed well enough to defeat both the XF-93A and the XF-90. However, by this stage the USAF's funding priorities had changed and the XF-88 became surplus to requirements. Nevertheless, McDonnell upgraded the first XF-88 to XF-88A standard then modified it again as a test aircraft for the Allison XT38A turboprop engine – giving it a nose mounted propeller – while retaining its two J34 turbojets. This gas-guzzling triple engine configuration was designated XF-88B and first flew on April 14, 1953.

Meanwhile, combat experience in Korea had demonstrated a renewed need for a long-range bomber escort fighter. A request for designs was issued in early 1951 and proposals were tendered by Republic, Northrop, North American, Lockheed and McDonnell. The latter's entry was a thoroughly revised XF-88 and the USAF accepted it in May 1951.

The new designation F-101 was applied but McDonnell opted to transfer the Voodoo name over from the earlier design. The work done up

F-101B-105-MC VOODOO (58-0267) ▼

Phoenix Air Defense Sector, 15th Fighter-Interceptor Squadron, 1961. This aircraft would serve with the USAF for a long time until it was finally sent to MASDC on November 19, 1980.

to this point on the XF-88 had been part of the company's bid and now it was possible to get a head start on development by using the XF-88A prototype to test components destined for the new aircraft.

It was given a T-tail with all-moving tailplane, splitter plates for its wingroot intakes and most significantly – Pratt & Whitney J57-P-13 turbojets with 11,700lb-ft of thrust each. Although the modified aircraft was now nearly twice as heavy, going from a combined thrust of 7200lb-ft to 23,400lb-ft promised a dramatic improvement in performance.

Armament was now a quartet of Colt M39 20mm revolver cannon and a centreline hardpoint could carry a nuclear bomb. The MA-7 fire control system, including an AN/APS-54 radar and MA-2 bombing computer (aka Low Altitude Bombing System – LABS), was fitted.

In late 1953, the USAF issued a request for proposals with the specification Weapons System 217A for a supersonic two-seater interceptor to replace the Northrop F-89 Scorpion. It had been hoped that the F-102B Delta Dagger would fulfil this role but that type was suffering protracted delays. The three front-running entries were a variant of the F-100 from North American, a swept-wing Scorpion from Northrop and a two-seater F-101 from McDonnell.

Even before the F-101A's first flight, the USAF gave McDonnell a contract for a reconnaissance version of the type under Weapons System 105L. This was intended to replace the Air Force's aging Republic RF-84F Thunderflashes. A mock-up of the resulting design, dubbed the 'YRF-101A', was inspected on January 13, 1954. The F-101's enormous airframe was well suited to conversion as a reconnaissance platform – armament was deleted and a longer nose was added to accommodate four film cameras for low-level photography plus two vertical cameras for high-altitude work which were positioned where the ammo boxes

F-101B-110-MC VOODOO (58-0336) ▽

Great Falls Air Defense Sector, 29th Fighter-Interceptor Squadron, 1965. This aircraft was serving with the Air Defense Weapons Center in 1980 but little is known of its fate after that. It was likely sent to MASDC.

Mcdonnell F-101 Voodoo

for the cannon had been. The nose cameras all sat on a tray which could be easily lowered down for servicing.

In June 1954, the USAF chose the two-seater F-101 as its Scorpion replacement – under the designation F-101B. In order to accommodate the pilot and weapon systems operator seated in tandem, the F-101B featured an all-new forward fuselage with both crew seated beneath a single clamshell canopy. The F-101B also had more powerful engines – two J57-P-55 turbojets with 11,990lb-ft thrust each.

Armament was four Falcon air-to-air missiles carried in a weapons bay, with the F-101A's cannon being deleted. Later F-101Bs would be able to carry two unguided MB-1 Genie nuclear rockets instead.

The first F-101A flew on September 29, 1954, at Edwards Air Force Base with McDonnell chief test pilot Robert C Little at the controls and effortlessly went supersonic – the first time an aircraft had done this on its first test flight. An F-100 flying chase was unable to keep up even with its afterburners on.

Despite the requirement for a long-range escort fighter having now been dropped for a second time, the USAF ordered 77 F-101As, the type now being referred to as a 'tactical fighter'. The first of two YRF-101A prototypes (the 16th and 17th F-101A airframes having been set aside for conversion to the reconnaissance configuration) flew on June 30, 1955, and the first flight of the NF-101B two-seater prototype took place on March 27, 1957.

Delivery of the first production spec F-101A, to the 27th Strategic Fighter

F-101B-70-MC VOODOO (56-0271) ▼

Detroit Air Defense Sector, 87th Fighter-Interceptor Squadron, 1965. This aircraft had an unusually short term service with the USAF. It was sent to MASDC in March 1968 where it remained until scrapped in May 1977.

F-101B-91-MC VOODOO (57-0348) ▼

Washington Air Defense Sector, 444th Fighter-Interceptor Squadron, 1967. The 444th FIS operated the Voodoo until 1968 when the squadron was inactivated. Its aircraft were then assigned to ANG units. 57-0348 would serve with the North Dakota ANG and Texas ANG before being sent to MASDC in June 1982. It was one of the last active Voodoos in USAF service.

Wing, took place in May 1957 and most of the aircraft ordered were deployed to bases in Europe. USAF pilots soon discovered that the Voodoo had a nasty tendency to pitch up at high speed resulting from its small wings and T-tail. Another problem was the type's structural weakness – it was unable to handle loads of more than 6.33 g, even though the USAF had specified 7.33 g. And the aircraft's forwards-retracting nosewheel also caused difficulties. If it had not been retracted before the aircraft hit 90mph, the gear hydraulics were too weak to overcome the resulting aerodynamic drag and the nosewheel stayed down.

In order to cure the structural problem, McDonnell hastily produced a strengthened version of the F-101A as the F-101C, with just 47 being built and following immediately after the 77 F-101As on the production line. Meanwhile, deliveries of the RF-101A to the 17th Tactical Reconnaissance Squadron of the 363rd Tactical Reconnaissance Wing began on May 6, 1957 – the new aircraft replacing RB-57A/B Canberras and becoming the USAF's first supersonic reconnaissance platform. A total of 35 RF-101As were delivered from May to October 1957, with production then switching to the F-101C-based RF-101C. A further 166 of these were made.

In July 1957, the 27th Strategic Fighter Wing was transferred to Tactical Air Command and became the 27th Fighter-Bomber Wing (27th FBW). The F-101A was now repurposed as a nuclear bomber.

BREAKING RECORDS

The early Voodoos may have had their drawbacks but they were nevertheless eye-wateringly quick. With this in mind, the USAF was eager to use the aircraft to set some new records. An ambitious attempt to establish new transcontinental speed records took place on November 27, 1957, under the moniker Operation Sun-Run. Six brand new RF-101Cs were prepared for the attempt, which was to see two flying from Los Angeles to New York and back while another two flew one-

Mcdonnell F-101 Voodoo

way from Los Angeles to New York. Each team also had a backup aircraft in case any problems arose with the primary two.

The success or failure of the operation depended heavily on the USAF's first jet-propelled tanker – the Boeing KC-135A Stratotanker – for a total of 26 in-flight refuellings. On the day, the aircraft took off from Ontario International Airport in California, and flew to McGuire AFB in New Jersey. Two landed at McGuire

while the other primary pair returned to California – landing at March AFB. The two backups dropped out when it became clear that the four primary aircraft were flying as expected.

By the time the operation concluded, 1st Lieutenant Gustav Klatt had set a new eastbound coast-to-coast record of three hours, seven minutes and 43 seconds at an average speed of 781.7mph. Captain Robert Sweet had

set a new westbound coast-to-coast record of three hours, 36 minutes and 33 seconds at an average speed of 677.77mph. He also set a new round trip record of six hours, 46 minutes and 36 seconds with an average speed of 721.85mph.

On December 12, 1957, Major Adrian Drew of the 27th FBW flew an F-101A fitted with J57-P-53 engines to a record-breaking 1207.6mph.

RF-101C-70-MC VOODOO (56-0097) ▼

66th Tactical Reconnaissance Wing, 17th Tactical Reconnaissance Squadron, 1965. The 66th TFW was stationed at RAF Upper Hayford throughout the late 60s, as a part of the forward deployed force in Europe. 56-0097 had a long career in the USAF and wouldn't go into storage at the MASDC until January 1979.

IN SERVICE AND FOREIGN USERS

The F-101C began entering service with the 27th FBW in 1958. The reconnaissance variant, the RF-101C, entered service in June 1958 and deliveries of the two-seater F-101B commenced on January 5, 1959, to the 60th Fighter-Interceptor Squadron. Production continued into 1961 for a total of 479 F-101Bs built. Seventy-nine of them were fitted with dual controls as trainers under the designation TF-101B and a further 152 were later retrofitted with dual controls – all these aircraft being designated TF-101F then F-101F

(the F-101D and F-101E designations having been applied to proposed J79 engined variants which were never built). All were also fully combat-capable. Some F-101Bs continued in US service into the early 1980s before being retired.

In USAF service, the RF-101A and C aircraft of the 363rd Tactical Reconnaissance Wing flew missions over Cuba during the Cuban Missile Crisis, starting on October 23, 1962. The RF-101C was then deployed to Vietnam with the 67th Tactical Reconnaissance Wing in 1964. The type flew more than

35,000 sorties and 39 aircraft were lost, 33 of them in combat. Five of these were hit by SAMs, one was destroyed when a US airfield was attacked and another was shot down by a MiG-21 in September 1967. ALQ-71 ECM pods were carried by RF-101Cs from April 1967 to provide some protection from SAMs but the increased drag slowed the aircraft to the point where it became more vulnerable to fighter attack. The type, which was the only USAF F-101 variant to see combat, had been withdrawn and replaced by the RF-4C Phantom II by November 1970.

▼ RF-101A-30-MC VOODOO (54-1516)

363rd Tactical Reconnaissance Wing, 1962. The 363rd TRW was assigned to Shaw AFB in South Carolina. However, as tensions rose with nuclear missiles being shipped to Cuba in the autumn of 1962, detachments from the 363rd were deployed in Florida. From here, low level photo reconnaissance missions were conducted over the Cuban mainland. 54-1516 was among the aircraft that overflew Cuba on those dangerous, high priority missions.

Mcdonnell F-101 Voodoo

RF-101C-40-MC VOODOO (56-0163) SUN-RUN #1 ▽

363rd Tactical Reconnaissance Wing, November 27, 1957. Operation Sun-Run, involving six individually numbered RF-101Cs, was an attempt to break transcontinental speed records. This aircraft was flow by Captain Ray Schrecengost and was in the first wave of aircraft set to break the Los Angeles-New York-Los Angeles speed record. The time for this round trip for Sun-Run #1 was 7:17.07. 56-0163 was struck off charge on September 15, 1965.

RF-101C-40-MC VOODOO (56-0164) SUN-RUN #2 ▽

363rd Tactical Reconnaissance Wing, November 27, 1957. This aircraft was part of the second wave set to break the Los Angeles-New York speed record, flown by Captain Robert Kilpatrick. This flight encountered problems in finding one of the tankers (the one-way aircraft had to refuel four times, and the round trip required eight refuelling cycles). The trip was made in 3:11.59. Despite the refuelling difficulties, the trip was completed four minutes faster than Sun Run #1. 56-0164 was written off on October 10, 1960, in unknown circumstances.

RF-101C-40-MC VOODOO (56-0165) SUN-RUN #3 ▽

363rd Tactical Reconnaissance Wing, November 27, 1957. This aircraft served as a spare for the first wave of Operation Sun-Run. Captain Don Hawkins recorded the fastest time to the first tanker of all the first wave aircraft. But since neither #1 nor #2 had encountered problems Sun-Run #3 diverted to March AFB and was out of the race. The aircraft remained in USAF service and served in Vietnam with the 20th TRS. It was hit by ground fire on December 5, 1966, and crashed near Yen Bai AB.

60163

FB-163

60164

FB-164

60165

FB-165

Mcdonnell F-101 Voodoo

RF-101C-40-MC VOODOO (56-0166) SUN-RUN #4

363rd Tactical Reconnaissance Wing, November 27, 1957. The first aircraft of the Sun-Run second wave, it was flown by Captain Robert Sweet, who would set a new speed record for a round trip flight: Los Angeles-New York-Los Angeles in 6:46.36. This aircraft is preserved at the Wright-Patterson AFB museum.

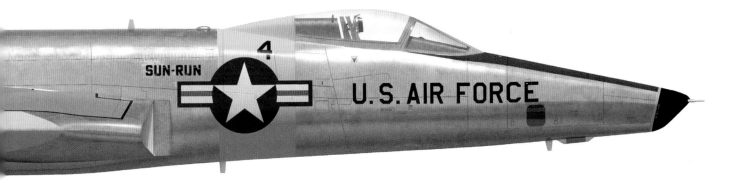

RF-101C-40-MC VOODOO (56-0167) SUN-RUN #5

363rd Tactical Reconnaissance Wing, November 27, 1957. Despite controller problems which lead to difficulties in finding one of the tankers, Captain Gustav R Klatt managed to set a new transcontinental speed record of 3:07.43, beating Major John Glenn's previous record by nearly 14 minutes (set in an F8U-1P Crusader). This aircraft was written off on July 24, 1964.

RF-101C-40-MC VOODOO (56-0168) SUN-RUN #6

363rd Tactical Reconnaissance Wing, November 27, 1957. Second wave spare aircraft flown by Captain Robert Buckhart. As #4 and #5 didn't encounter problems, this aircraft diverted to March AFB after the first refuelling. It was struck off charge in October 1974 after serving with the Mississippi ANG.

Mcdonnell F-101 Voodoo

RF-101C-60-MC VOODOO (54-0041) ▼

460th Tactical Reconnaissance Wing, 45th Tactical Reconnaissance
Squadron, 1969. 54-0041 survived deployment in the Vietnam War and
would eventually be transferred to the 153rd Tactical Reconnaissance
Squadron, which was part of the Mississippi ANG. The aircraft was send
to AMARC in February 1974 and eventually scrapped in November 1984.

RF-101C-40-MC VOODOO (56-0166) ▼

186th Tactical Reconnaissance Group, 153rd Tactical Reconnaissance Squadron,
Mississippi ANG, 1977. This aircraft was #4 in the famous Operation Sun-Run –
illustrated elsewhere in this chapter. Its last assignment, however, was with the
Mississippi ANG, where it would serve until it was struck off duty. This aircraft is
preserved at the Wright-Patterson AFB museum.

▼ RF-101C-55-MC VOODOO (56-0165)

18th Tactical Fighter Wing, 15th Tactical Reconnaissance Squadron, 1965. Having served as aircraft #3 in Operation Sun-Run, 56-0165 was shot down near Yen Bai AB in Vietnam on December 5, 1966, while serving with the 20th TRS. The pilot, Captain Arthur L Warren, ejected and remained in contact with the USAF for two hours, reporting that he was under fire. Contact was lost 20 minutes before the arrival of the SAR team and never regained. Extraction could not be attempted due to intense ground fire in the area. Warren's remains were recovered on September 17, 1986, and he was buried at the Arlington National Cemetery.

Mcdonnell F-101 Voodoo

Meanwhile, surviving F-101As had been withdrawn from service starting in 1966, although 29 were converted into reconnaissance machines for the ANG with a modified camera nose being fitted, under the designation RF-101G. The remaining two-seater F-101Bs were withdrawn from front-line service between 1969 and 1972, continuing

to serve with the ANG until 1982. The F-101C was replaced with the Phantom F-4C during 1966, having never seen combat, although 32 were converted to serve as ANG reconnaissance machines under the designation RF-101H – which they did up to 1972.

Following the cancellation of the Avro Canada CF-105 Arrow in 1959,

the Canadian Royal Air Force required a replacement for its ageing fleet of CF-100 Canucks. Canada was subsequently able to reach an agreement with the US for the supply of 56 ex-USAF F-101Bs and 10 F-101Fs – which became known as the CF-101B and CF-101F respectively.

The Republic of China Air Force received eight ex-USAF RF-101As in

RF-101G-30-MC VOODOO (54-1462) ▽

123rd Tactical Reconnaissance Wing, 165th Tactical Reconnaissance Squadron, Kentucky ANG, 1971. This aircraft started out as an F-101A Voodoo but had its radar and cannon replaced by cameras in 1966. It was one of 29 F-101As to undergo conversion to RF-101G and like the others would be operated by ANG units. Their service career was short however, and this aircraft would be transferred into MASDC storage in 1972. It was scrapped in 1975.

1959 and used them for overflights of mainland China during the 1960s – with three apparently being shot down during these hazardous missions, two by MiGs and one by AAA fire. The surviving ROCAF RF-101As were retired during the late 1970s.

Between 1970 and 1971, 46 surviving Canadian F-101s were returned to the US in exchange for 56 upgraded F-101Bs and 10 F-101Fs under a programme dubbed 'Peace Wings'. These remained in service into the early 80s before being replaced with CF/A-18A/B Hornets. Two

further F-101Bs were leased from the US by Canada in 1982 – one being converted into an electronic warfare training aircraft under the designation EF-101B and the other being retained in its original configuration as a flight proficiency trainer for the EF-101B. Both were returned to the US five years later.

A total of 807 examples were built.

▼ RF-101B-115-MC VOODOO (58-0434)

152nd Tactical Reconnaissance Group, 192nd Tactical Reconnaissance Squadron, Nevada ANG, 1972. This aircraft had a particularly colourful history. In April 1962 it was transferred to the RCAF as 17434, only to be returned to the USAF in May 1971. It was then converted to RF-101B standard and put into service with the 192nd TRS, the only unit to operate the RF-101B model. The RF-101B proved very time consuming to maintain, so this and the other RF-101Bs were put in to storage at the AMARC in June 1975 before being scrapped in January 1980.

F-101B-105MC VOODOO (58-0273)

119th Fighter-Interceptor Group, 178th Fighter-Interceptor Squadron, North Dakota ANG, 1975. This aircraft was flown to AMARC in July 1982 while serving with the 111th FIS.

F-101B-85-MC VOODOO (57-0295)

141st Fighter Group, 116th Fighter-Interceptor Squadron, Washington ANG, 1973. This aircraft was send to AMARC in August 1976 and eventually scrapped in November 1984.

F-101B-105MC VOODOO (58-0276)

147th Fighter-Interceptor Group, 111th Fighter-Interceptor Squadron, Texas ANG, 1982. The last active Voodoo unit in the USAF was the 111th FIS and this is how the aircraft appeared at the time. It is seen sporting markings indicating that the unit won the William Tell trophy in 1978 and 1980. Since this was the last active Voodoo unit, the aircraft was sent to MASDC when the 147th FIG traded its Voodoos for Phantoms. This aircraft is currently preserved at Robins AFB, Georgia.

Mcdonnell F-101 Voodoo

CF-101B VOODOO (101043) (EX-USAF F-101B-95-MC VOODOO, 57-0380) ▼

416 Squadron, RCAF, 1984. This aircraft went into service with the RCAF in September 1971 and was transferred to 425 Sqn. At the end of its career it was serving with the 416 Sqn, before being struck off charge on May 24, 1985. This aircraft is currently on display at the Atlantic Canada Aviation Museum, Halifax, Nova Scotia.

RF-101A-35-MC VOODOO (54-1519) ▼

4th Composite Reconnaissance Squadron, Republic of China Air Force, 1960. Four RF-101As were delivered to the ROCAF from PACAF squadrons. This aircraft was eventually shot down over the Taiwan Strait on March 18, 1965, by a MiG-19.

CF-101B VOODOO (101050) (EX- USAF F-101B-95MC VOODOO, 57-0396)

409 Squadron, RCAF, 1982. This aircraft was transferred to the RCAF in October 1970 and served with the 416 and 425 Sqns before being struck off active duty and used for fire practice.

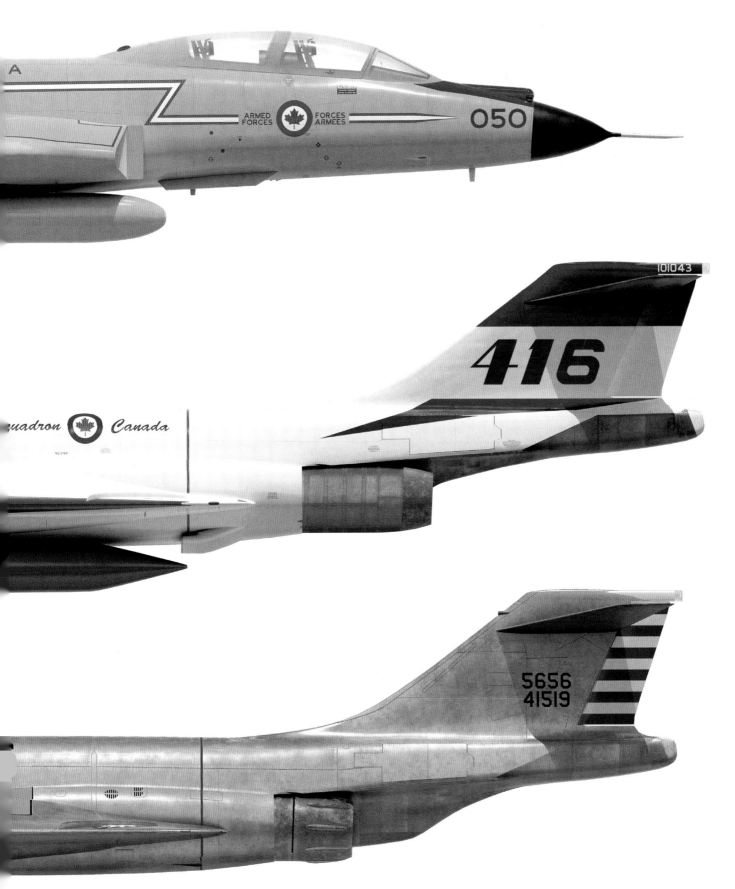

CONVAIR F-102 DELTA DAGGER

1953-1976

Intended to defend the United States against Soviet bombers, Convair's delta-winged F-102A interceptor pushed the boundaries of what was possible in the early 1950s and as such had a difficult development. Eventually the design would prove its worth as the excellent F-106 Delta Dart.

F-102A-50-CO DELTA DAGGER (54-3454)

325th Fighter Group, 317th Fighter-Interceptor Squadron, 1956. Almost fresh off the production line, this F-102 sports the original marking layout, which was very short-lived. The insignia on the nose and the U. S. Air Force stencil moved forward to almost the intake lip. The aircraft's intake layout dictated that the stencils had to be bent to fit. Also, notice the lack of an antiglare panel and walkway on the upper surface of the intake. This aircraft would be struck off charge in December 1972. While most Deuces were sent into storage a few years later, the early blocks (this is an aircraft from FY54) were usually written off before that could happen.

F-102A-55-CO DELTA DAGGER (56-1017)

Washington Air Defence Sector, 48th Fighter-Interceptor Squadron 'Tazlangian Devils', 1958. One of the most easily recognizable paint schemes ever worn by a Deuce. The white vertical stabilizer with dark green stars would be worn only while the squadron operated the F-102 – it was not carried over onto the F-106s that the squadron would later receive. 56-1017 was sent to AMARC as early as May 1970 but today is on display at the South Dakota Air and Space Museum at Ellisworth AFB.

Consolidated Vultee's Vultee Division had begun to examine the possibilities of a swept-wing aircraft during the Second World War – as well as the potential of rocket motors and ramjets. So when the USAAF issued a requirement for a supersonic point-defence interceptor in August 1945, the company responded with a swept-wing rocket-propelled design on October 13, 1945.

As work progressed into 1946, the company switched to a delta-wing layout. Ralph Schick, chief of aerodynamic research, met Messerschmitt Me 163 designer Alexander Lippisch at Wright-Patterson Air Force Base while this work was ongoing and the latter convinced

him that he had selected the correct layout for a supersonic interceptor. The design Schick and his team focused on, Model 7002, was powered by a single Westinghouse J30 jet engine with 1560lb-ft thrust plus six liquid-fuelled rockets providing 2000lb-ft of thrust each. A huge intake at the front of the aircraft would feed not only the J30 but would also pass air to the rockets' exhaust, augmenting their thrust. The duct was so large that there was no room for a conventional cockpit – therefore, the cockpit had to be positioned in a cone within the centre of the duct.

Remarkably, with hindsight, the USAAF accepted this design for development in November 1946 as the XP-92 after

inspecting a mockup. A flight demonstrator was required, so Consolidated Vultee put one together using existing components wherever possible – including a tricycle undercarriage composed of the nose gear from a Bell P-63 Kingcobra with the main gear from a North American FJ-1 Fury. Power came from a single non-afterburning Allison J33-A-21 turbojet with 4250lb-ft of thrust. The delta wings had a 60-degree sweepback and a large triangular tailfin took up most of the space on the spine of the aircraft.

In contrast to the mock-up design, a conventional cockpit was installed just ahead of the wings. The vehicle was completed in early 1948 – by which time the project had already been cancelled since there was no longer a perceived

Convair F-102 Delta Dagger

F-102A-60-CO DELTA DAGGER (56-1100) ▽

Detroit Air Defense Sector, 87th Fighter-Interceptor Squadron, 1959. For unknown reasons, this aircraft was sent to AMARC as early as November 1969. It would remain there until it was scrapped in 1977.

F-102A-80-CO DELTA DAGGER (56-1444) ▽

328th Fighter Group, 326th Fighter-Interceptor Squadron 'Skywolves', 1959. Like the 175th FIS of the South Dakota ANG, the 326th FIS painted the radomes of their F-102s. Another feature common for this period was the wing tanks being kept in Natural Metal finish. This aircraft would end up serving in the 509th FIS in Vietnam and was salvaged in July 1970 at Itazuke AB.

▼ F-102A-65-CO DELTA DAGGER (56-1184)

4727th Air Defence Group, 27th Fighter-Interceptor Squadron 'Fighting Eagles', 1958. The 27th Fighter Squadron is the oldest fighter squadron in the USAF, having been active since May 8, 1917. 56-1184 was also in service for a long time, being put into storage in March 1975, only to be resurrected in July 1978 as a PQM-102A target drone.

Convair F-102 Delta Dagger

need for a short-range point-defence interceptor of this type. Instead, the USAF had begun to consider a larger and more advanced supersonic interceptor – capable of much greater range and equipped with both a fire control system (FCS) and guided air-to-air missiles.

Even so, the delta wing concept continued to interest the Air Force and flight testing commenced on June 8, 1948, at Muroc Dry Lake – later to

become Edwards Air Force Base. The aircraft, now redesignated XF-92A, was first flown by Convair test pilot Ellis D 'Sam' Shannon. After 47 flights and 20 hours 33 minutes in the air, the XF-92A was handed over to the USAF on August 26, 1949, and further testing commenced with pilots Frank Everest and Chuck Yeager putting it through its paces. The USAF pilots found that the delta had unusual

handling properties, being very difficult to stall in a nose-up attitude.

In January 1950, the USAF finally issued Weapon System 201A, which crystalised its requirement for a missile-armed interceptor – later to be known as the '1954 interceptor' due to its anticipated delivery date. No fewer than 18 companies submitted proposals, with Convair offering a delta-winged concept which resembled a scaled-up XF-92A with a new fuselage forward of the wing including a solid nose to house the necessary radar and side intakes for the engine.

The 18 were whittled down to six semi-finalists offering nine different designs between them in May 1950 – Republic with three, North American with two, and Lockheed, Douglas, Chance-Vought and Convair with one each. Hughes won the contract to supply the FCS, under project MX-1179, the following month. This would eventually be known as the MA-1. The six semi-finalists became three in July 1951 – Convair, Lockheed and Republic – before Lockheed dropped out (or had its design cancelled – accounts vary as to exactly how Lockheed left

the contest). Republic's design was chosen to proceed to mock-up stage as the XF-103, discussed elsewhere in this publication, while Convair's design would also proceed as the XF-102.

Having had its mock-up approved, Convair was commissioned to build a pair of YF-102 prototypes. Hughes was making very slow progress with the advanced MA-1, so in November 1952 it was decided that the F-102A would be fitted with the Hughes E-9 FCS as an interim measure – it was thought that this would be more readily available since it amounted to an upgraded version of

F-102A-40-CO DELTA DAGGER (54-1405)

86th Fighter-Interceptor Group, 496th Fighter-Interceptor Squadron, 1960. Another colourful Deuce, this one with the addition of stripes around the nose, indicating that it was assigned to the squadron CO. This aircraft is currently preserved at Ashland, NE.

F-102A-75-CO DELTA DAGGER (56-1423)

327th Fighter Group, 61st Fighter-Interceptor Squadron 'Top Dogs', 1960. This aircraft would be transferred to the Pennsylvania ANG in 1962, but would only serve there for a few month as it crashed on approach on October 29, 1962.

Convair F-102 Delta Dagger

F-102A-51-CO DELTA DAGGER (56-0960) ▼

39th Air Division, 4th Fighter-Interceptor Squadron 'Fighting Fuujins', 1961. The red fuselage stripes on the 'Red-Striped Rascal' indicate that this aircraft was assigned to the CO of the 4th FIS. This aircraft was sent to AMARC in May 1970 and scrapped five years later in 1975.

the E-4 FCS already being used by the F-86D. The MA-1 would be reserved for a future version of the F-102, to be known as the F-102B, with the F-102A receiving the E-9 (later the MG-3).

Meanwhile, the XF-92A had been refitted with a 7500lb-ft thrust Allison J33-A-29 engine, requiring a significant fuselage extension to the rear. Flight testing of the aircraft continued into 1953, now under the auspices of NACA, and although its performance proved

disappointing even with the new engine, the XF-92A was crucial in helping to amass huge quantities of data for the F-102 programme.

The first YF-102 made its flight debut on October 24, 1953, flown by test pilot Richard L Johnson. It bore a strong resemblance to the XF-92A from the forward wingroots back, having a pure delta wing with 60-degree sweepback, large fin and no tailplanes. The tricycle undercarriage mainwheels retracted

inwards towards the fuselage and the nosewheel retracted forwards. The engine was a single Pratt & Whitney J57-P-11 with 10,900lb-ft of thrust. No space had been made available to fit a cannon because the production version of the aircraft was to be armed exclusively with missiles – six Hughes Falcons.

On November 2, just nine days after its first flight, the YF-102 was wrecked in an accident. The aircraft's engine flamed out on take-off, leaving Johnson no choice

F-102A-90-CO DELTA DAGGER (57-0799)

327th Fighter Group, 325th Fighter-Interceptor Squadron, 1962. This aircraft was salvaged at Naha AB in June 1971, which could indicate that it served time in the Vietnam war and had sustained battle damage. It was decided not to bring this aircraft back to CONUS after its tour overseas.

but to put the aircraft back down again hard. The pilot was badly injured in the ensuing crash.

Testing resumed on January 11, 1954, with the second YF-102, now flown by Sam Shannon. Tests quickly showed that the aircraft was severely underpowered, could not reach supersonic speeds and handled poorly. In short, it was a 'dud'. Convair's mortified engineers immediately went back to the drawing board to find ways of resolving the aircraft's issues.

Reputedly, within the space of 117 days they came up with a host of fixes which, taken together, formed the YF-102A. Among the changes were the installation of the more powerful J57-P-23 engine with 12,000lb-ft of thrust, a canopy redesign, a 7ft longer 'area-ruled' or 'Coke bottle' fuselage shape and a cambered wing.

Area ruling, discovered by NACA's Richard T Whitcomb in 1951, amounted to the idea that changes in an aircraft's cross section should be as gradual as

possible, allowing air to flow smoothly over the whole machine, rather than particular individual parts of it. Changing the YF-102A's fuselage shape prevented a 'bunching' of air, a phenomenon which on the YF-102 had caused progressively increasing drag approaching Mach 1. Pilots found that the YF-102A needed less runway to take off, could manage Mach 1.2 in level flight and had a superior high-altitude performance to that of the YF-102.

Convair F-102 Delta Dagger

F-102A-55-CO DELTA DAGGER (56-1014) ▽

86th Air Division, 32nd Fighter-Interceptor Squadron 'Wolfhounds', 1966. This aircraft served with a number of different squadrons throughout its career. From 1960-1969 it was deployed at Soesterberg Air Base in Holland, while serving with the 32nd FIS. The aircraft was struck off charge in November 1974 and sent to AMARC, only to be converted into a PQM-102A drone. It was shot down over the Gulf of Mexico on August 8, 1978.

F-102A-75-CO DELTA DAGGER (56-1314) ▽

Air Forces Iceland, 57th Fighter-Interceptor Squadron 'Black Knights', 1972. Most F-102s were serving with ANG units by the early 1970s, but the Deuces of the 57th FIS would soldier on for a few more years. At the time, aircraft serving in arctic regions would have large parts of the fuselage, wings and stabilisers painted Day-Glo orange. Air Forces Iceland was no exception. As with many other F-102s, this aircraft was put into storage in the mid-70s (specifically, August 1974) and later converted into a PQM-102B. It then served until it was shot down during missile tests.

▼ F-102A-75-CO DELTA DAGGER (56-1319)

4780th Air Defence Wing, 1962. The 4780th ADW had responsibility for training the crews of F-102, F-106 and B-58 units and as such had the largest fleet of F-102s and TF-102s in the USAF. During the Cuban missile crisis the unit's interceptors were put on five-minute alert, and thus the unit was also part of the air defence of the CONUS. Like so many of F-102s, this aircraft would be converted into a PQM-102A and eventually shot down in a missile test on March 2, 1981.

Convair F-102 Delta Dagger

▼ F-102A-80-CO DELTA DAGGER (56-1470)

51st Fighter-Interceptor Wing, 82nd Fighter-Interceptor Squadron, 1966. The 82nd FIS was the last Delta Dagger unit in the PACAF before its deactivation in 1971. Its aircraft were left behind at Japanese bases and this one was salvaged at Naha AB in March 1971. It had served both in Vietnam and during the 1968 USS Pueblo crisis on the Korean peninsula.

F-102A-80-CO DELTA DAGGER (56-1420) ▼

405th Fighter Wing, 64th Fighter-Interceptor Squadron 'Scorpions', 1969. A few F-102 units would serve in operations over Vietnam. The 64th FIS was one of them. While stationed at Clark AFB in the Philippines, the squadron would rotate flights to bases in Vietnam and Thailand. Aircraft operating in the SEA theatre would receive the standard SEA camo scheme seen here. 56-1420 would be struck off charge in July 1970 at Itazuke AFB in Japan.

Even as Convair was struggling with the airframe, Hughes was encountering difficulties with the MG-3 FCS, which was proving to be more problematic that initially expected. Even though the first production spec F-102A's first flight was on June 24, 1955, the FCS wasn't ready – and the aircraft still could not achieve the required level of performance. Flutter was an issue when flying faster than Mach 1.2 and it took extensive further testing, plus a host of detail changes, before the aircraft was able to reach Mach 1.5 without difficulties.

From the initial production batch of F-102As, the 23rd example was given an enlarged fin – 11ft 6in compared to the original 8ft 8in – and this became a feature of the production model going forward.

A two-seat trainer variant, the TF-102A, took its maiden flight on October 31, 1955. Unusually, the TF-102A had its seats positioned side-by-side rather than in tandem – a feature which significantly improved communication between instructor and student. However, this configuration also made heavily revised engine intakes necessary, produced performance-degrading drag and required vortex generators to prevent buffeting.

USAF Air Defense Command (ADC) finally received its first '1954 Interceptor' in April 1956. The standard F-102A was made primarily of

Convair F-102 Delta Dagger

F-102A-65-CO DELTA DAGGER (56-1223) ▼

106th Fighter-Interceptor Group, 102nd Fighter-Interceptor Squadron,
New York ANG, 1974. The Deuces of the NY ANG were unusual in not
changing their markings when their ADC grey scheme was repainted in
SEA camo pattern. This resulted in these unique markings, distinguishing
this unit from most other F-102 units. The story of 56-1223 is otherwise
quite ordinary for a Deuce: In September 1974 it was sent into storage at
AMARC, only to be converted into a PQM-102B in July 1979.

TF-102A-41-CO DELTA DAGGER (56-2347) ▼

147th Fighter-Interceptor Group, 111th Fighter-Interceptor Squadron, Texas
ANG, 1972. While many F-102 squadrons sported some very fancy markings,
the 111th FIS had a much more subtle approach. This particular aircraft
would most likely have been flown on more than one occasion by the future
President George Walker Bush, who served with the 111th in the late 60s to
early 70s. The aircraft was withdrawn from service in December 1973.

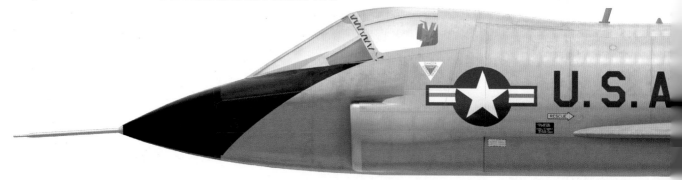

F-102A-80-CO DELTA DAGGER (56-1436)

405th Fighter Wing, 509th Fighter-Interceptor Squadron, 1969. This F-102 were stationed at Udorn RTAFB and provided top cover for USAF B-52 Arc Light missions over Vietnam. While this particular aircraft was not shot down during these missions, the F-102 loss rate was high and the type had been withdrawn from Vietnam by early 1970. Along with the rest of the 509th FIS, this aircraft went to Japan where most if not all aircraft of the squadron were salvaged.

Convair F-102 Delta Dagger

aluminium alloy but with some limited use of titanium. It was powered by a single Pratt & Whitney J57-23A or J57-25 turbojet providing 11,700lb-ft of dry thrust or a healthier 17,200lb-ft with afterburner. Its intakes had splitter plates to reduce airflow turbulence and four fuel tanks provided a total capacity

of 1085 US gallons. No provision was made for external tanks initially.

It could carry six Hughes Falcons – a pair in each of three internal weapons bays. When needed, the missiles were lowered from their bays on launch rails before firing. In addition, the F-102A could carry 24 2.75in folding-fin air

rockets (FFARS) in tubes that were built into the weapons bay doors.

The first unit to receive the F-102A was the 327th Fighter-Interceptor Squadron at George Air Force Base in California and the type would go on to equip numerous units both with the USAF and ANG. Service personnel tended to

T-102A-90-CO DELTA DAGGER (57-0847) ▽

112th Fighter-Interceptor Group, 146th Fighter-Interceptor Squadron, Pennsylvania ANG, 1974. Being from the FY57, this aircraft was one of the last Deuces produced, but its story is similar to that of many of the other F-102s produced. It was put into storage at the AMARC bone yard and a few years later resurrected as a PQM-102A. 57-0847 was shot down on August 28, 1979, over the White Sands test range.

61414

FLA. AIR

refer to it as the 'Deuce' rather than by its formal 'Delta Dagger' name.

During 1958, Deuces were retrofitted with a drop tank under each wing to improve range. Provision would later be made for an inflight refuelling probe which could also be installed or removed as needed. No other external stores were carried by F-102As.

And during the early 1960s, the F-102A fleet was upgraded to carry the AIM-26A Nuclear Falcon missile internally. Carrying the bulky Nuclear Falcon meant that the number of FFARs that could be carried was reduced. The latter would eventually be deleted from the design altogether. While its primary role would be the defence of the continental United States, the F-102A also operated in West Germany, Iceland and South Korea. A number of F-102 units were deployed to South East Asia in 1962 to intercept any Soviet-supplied jet bombers that might be deployed by

F-102A-75-CO DELTA DAGGER (56-1414)

125th Fighter-Interceptor Group, 159th Fighter-Interceptor Squadron 'The Boxin' Gators', Florida ANG, 1962. This aircraft would operate in the Florida ANG for almost its entire period of service. The aircraft caught fire and crashed on May 18, 1967, near Jacksonville APT.

Convair F-102 Delta Dagger

F-102A-80-CO DELTA DAGGER (56-1502) ▼

119th Fighter-Interceptor Group, 178th Fighter-Interceptor Squadron 'Happy Hooligans', North Dakota ANG, 1968. This is one of the few F-102s that was not converted into a target drone and destroyed in testing or training. It was instead preserved at Fargo APT, but marked with the serial number 53432.

F-102A-50-CO DELTA DAGGER (55-3427) ▼

124th Fighter Group, 190th Fighter-Interceptor Squadron, Idaho ANG, 1968. The story of this F-102 is fairly typical: it began its career in the ADC, followed by a brief stint with the 4780th ADW, the main F-102 training wing at the time, before serving with various ANG units. In 1972 it was put into storage at AMARC, then converted into a PQM-102A in October 1975. It was destroyed in a missile test on December 12, 1978.

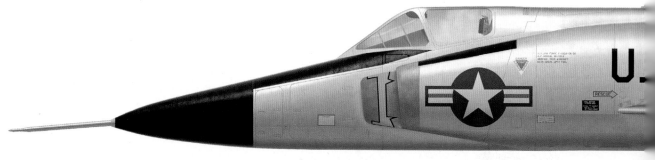

F-102A-65-CO DELTA DAGGER (56-1174)

114th Fighter-Interceptor Group, 175th Fighter-Interceptor Squadron, South Dakota ANG, 1963. The coloured radome sported by this aircraft is unusual but not unique. The same goes for the 'S.DAK.Air Guard' stencil that has replaced the usual U.S. Air Force marking on the aircraft's intake. This aircraft would have a relatively short service period before being put into storage in June 1970, while many ANG units were still operating the Deuce.

TF-102A-20-CO DELTA DAGGER (54-1367) ▼

163rd Fighter-Interceptor Group, 196th Fighter-Interceptor Squadron, California ANG, 1968. The Tub, as the trainer version of the F-102 was affectionately known, was produced in only small numbers but served with a wide range of Deuce-operating units. It wasn´t uncommon for a unit to have at least one or two Tubs in their inventory and the California ANG was no different. This aircraft would remain in service until January 1975 when it was sent to AMARC. It ended its days as a ground target at Biggs Army Airfield range in Texas.

▽ F-102A-60-CO DELTA DAGGER (56-1052)

342th Squ in the Hellenic Air Force, 1977. Greece was one of two air forces outside of the USAF that would operate the Delta Dagger. This aircraft served in various units in the USAF until 1969 when it was transferred to Greece. Today this aircraft is on display at Militaire Luchtvaart Museum at Soesterberg, Holland, marked with the serial number 56-1032.

▽ F-102A-45-CO DELTA DAGGER (55-3395)

191 Filo, Turkish Air Force, 1968. After serving with the USAF for roughly 12 years, this aircraft was transferred to the Turkish Air Force, where it would operate until mid-1979.

Convair F-102 Delta Dagger

▼ **PQM-102A-75-CO DELTA DAGGER (56-1376)**

6585th Test Group, 1981. Many of the F-102s put into storage at AMARC would be converted into PQM-102A target drones. This aircraft is one example. Most, if not all, of these would be lost over the Mexican Gulf during missile testing and this aircraft is no exception. It was destroyed on January 15, 1982, during its ninth mission as a drone.

North Vietnam – a possibility that was considered a credible threat at the time.

Two years later, on August 4, 1964, Deuces of the 509th Fighter-Interceptor Squadron flew from Clark Air Base in the Philippines to Da Nang Air Base. From here, they flew close support missions using 2.75in FFARs against targets in North Vietnam. During the mid-to-late 1960s, up to 1968, F-102As flew escort to B-52s during strike missions north of the border. At night, the F-102As were able to use their heat-seeking Falcons against enemy heat sources such as campfires, motorised vehicles and generators.

Eleven F-102As and a single TF-102A – a dozen Deuces in total – were lost during the war. Four of these were due to engine failures, three were destroyed on the ground (one when it collided with an RF-4 Phantom II and the other two due to enemy action), one was lost while being ferried, another crashed during a night landing and two were shot down by ground fire.

The 12th Deuce destroyed was the only one to be shot down by a North Vietnamese aircraft. This F-102A, flown by 1st Lieutenant Wallace Wiggins of the 509th Fighter-Interceptor Squadron, was escorting a B-52 during an Arc Light mission on February 3, 1968, at 36,000ft when an undetected MiG-21 fired an AA-2 Atoll heat-seeking missile at it. The missile did not explode immediately but lodged in the rear of the aircraft. As Wiggins and his flight leader flew on over Laos they were attacked by two more MiGs. Flight leader Major A I Lomax fired off three Falcon missiles and the MiGs withdrew – but when he looked for Wiggins, all he saw was a fireball and debris falling away. The missile lodged in the aircraft had eventually exploded and destroyed it; Wiggins was killed. The F-102A was withdrawn from Vietnam later that year.

The type continued to serve with

the USAF and Air National Guard units well into the 1970s. However, starting in 1973, the US government contracted Sperry Flight Systems and Fairchild Aircraft Corp to convert a large number of F-102As into unmanned target drones under the Pave Deuce Program. A pair of prototypes still capable of crewed operation – designated QF-102A – were converted, followed by a 'production' series designated PQM-102A. The first flight of a PQM-102A drone took place in August 1974 and the drones began to enter operational service two months later.

A standard PQM-102A could no longer be flown from the cockpit since much of that space was necessarily filled with the electronics needed for remote operation. Later on, F-102As were converted to PQM-102B standard, which featured improved systems and a radar altimeter which allowed them to be flown as low as 200ft. In addition, the electronics were relocated so that a pilot could fly a PQM-102B from the cockpit if required.

By the time the Pave Deuce Program ended, more than 200 F-102As had been converted into drones. These were mostly shot down by F-4s, F-106s and F-15s. Some were even used to test the Patriot missile system for the US Army.

The last one was apparently expended in 1985 and the type was succeeded by the North American/Sperry QF-100.

Around 35 F-102As and eight TF-102As were delivered to Turkey in 1968, which eventually retired them in 1979 – two having apparently been shot down by F-5s of the Hellenic Air Force during the invasion of Cyprus in 1974. In fact, at this time Greece was also operating the F-102A, having received 20 of them plus six TF-102As from the USAF in 1969. Like their Turkish opposite numbers, these were retired in 1979. The two nations' F-102As never met in combat.

In total, two YF-102As, 873 F-102As and 111 TF-102As were built, with the last F-102A being delivered in September 1958, for a total of 986 F-102s.

REPUBLIC XF-103 'THUNDERWARRIOR'

1950-1957

Starting out as a contemporary of the more realistic XF-102, Republic's XF-103 evolved into a Mach 4 titanium monster. The engineering challenges were enormous and the design was dropped before it became technologically feasible to build it.

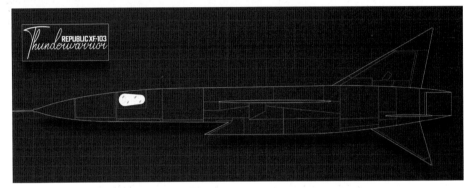

When the Soviet Union successfully tested its first atomic bomb on August 29, 1949, and resulting debris was collected and analysed by the US a few days later, it became clear that America was facing a new threat of hitherto unimaginable scale.

It had previously been revealed that the Soviets had reverse-engineered captured Boeing B-29 bombers to create the Tupolev Tu-4 and were building it in large numbers. This was already a grave cause for concern, since a Soviet B-29 would have sufficient range to reach the continental United States, albeit on a one-way mission. It took very little imagination, in the autumn of 1949, to picture wave after wave of red star-emblazoned nuclear bombers appearing in the skies over Chicago or Los Angeles and unleashing Armageddon.

Consequently, as mentioned in the previous chapter, the USAF issued Weapon System 201A in January 1950 for a missile-armed interceptor capable of knocking out as many Soviet bombers as possible before they could reach their targets. Eighteen companies put forward designs and six semi-finalists were chosen in May 1950 – these being reduced to just Convair, Lockheed and Republic in July 1951. Lockheed failed to make the final

cut and both Convair and Republic were given contracts to develop their aircraft as the XF-102 and XF-103 respectively.

The XF-102 was to be the USAF's answer to the Tu-4 and any subsequent subsonic jet bombers that might appear by 1954. But what if the Soviets were able to quickly develop a next-generation supersonic bomber? Meeting that threat would require an interceptor capable of truly outstanding high-speed performance.

Republic's AP-57, a development of a high-altitude interceptor proposal known as AP-44A three years earlier, was designed to offer that performance. Power would be provided by a Wright XJ67-W-3 turbojet – a licence-built version of the Bristol Olympus – which would develop 15,000lb-ft of dry thrust or 22,000lb-ft with afterburner, plus an XRJ55-W-1 ramjet with 18,800lb-ft of thrust. While only the turbojet could be used at take-off, when the correct altitude was reached the ramjet could be fired up to provide a combined output of more than 37,000lb-ft.

Both propulsion systems would have been fed by a single enormous ventral intake. The aircraft itself, made entirely from titanium to cope with the tremendous kinetic heating it would experience at Mach 4, looked more like a missile than a fighter. Its small wings, tailfin and tailplanes were all sharply triangular and although the pilot – the aircraft was a single-seater – sat in the forward fuselage there was no canopy. Instead, the pilot look ahead through a periscope with only side windows offering a direct view of the outside world. In place of the usual ejection system, there would be a survival capsule that could be jettisoned downwards in the event of an emergency.

Armament would be six Hughes Falcon air-to-air missiles housed in weapons bays on the sides of the fuselage plus 36 unguided rockets. There would be no cannon, no armour and no self-sealing fuel tanks, since interceptions would be taking place at speeds where such previously standard fighter components would be pointless.

Work on the XF-103 project proceeded slowly – understandable given the difficulties of designing an aircraft that was way beyond the state-of-the-art – and the mock-up was not ready for inspection until March 1953. Nevertheless, the mock-up was eventually approved and Republic was handed a contract for a trio of XF-103 prototypes in June 1954. By now however it was clear that working with titanium was extremely challenging and the J67 engine had fallen way behind schedule.

Work continued throughout 1955 and 1956. By January 1957, the design had been altered significantly – with the armament now being reduced to just four Falcons and no rockets. The USAF had clung to the idea of Republic's next generation interceptor for seven years but by now it had realised that the world had moved on and other, less ambitious, weapons systems were becoming available which might well do the same job as the XF-103 with much less difficulty and at a fraction of the cost.

In July 1957 the order for three prototype interceptors was reduced to an order for just one research aircraft. Then, on August 21, 1957, the entire XF-103 programme was cancelled. The design's nominal successor – the XF-108 (see elsewhere in this publication) – would ultimately suffer the same fate.

LOCKHEED F-104 STARFIGHTER

1956-2004

Designed as a response to the trend towards complex, heavy and expensive fighter aircraft, the simple, lightweight and relatively cheap F-104 could cruise above Mach 2 and fulfil a wide range of roles. It was exported and licence-built in huge numbers but suffered a high attrition rate due to frequent accidents.

During late 1951, Lockheed's chief designer Clarence L 'Kelly' Johnson hit upon the idea of a fast, lightweight and easy-to-build fighter based on the experiences of pilots fighting in the ongoing Korean War. As a private venture, he had his team examine a number of different configurations which might meet this goal.

Starting out with project L-242, the designers eventually fixed upon a workable configuration as L-246. This then became Model 83 – an aircraft form with distinctive short unswept wings, a long slender fuselage and T-tail. In the meantime, the USAF had issued weapon system requirement WS-303A in December 1952, calling for a new tactical day fighter capable of sustained supersonic performance.

Lockheed submitted Model 83 for consideration and a competition ensued, with other entries including Republic's AP-55 (an improved version of the XF-91 Thunderceptor prototype), North American's NA-212 and Northrop's N-102 Fang.

Model 83 was judged to be the most sophisticated and practical design, with the USAF ordering two XF-104 prototypes on March 12, 1953. Design work was completed on April 30 and it was decided that armament would be a 20mm General Electric Vulcan cannon plus two AIM-9B Sidewinder air-to-air missiles. The aircraft would be powered by General Electric's new J79 – although since this was unavailable at the time the Buick-built non-afterburning Wright J65-B-3, a licence-made copy of the British Armstrong-Siddeley Sapphire, would be used for the first prototypes.

Both completed XF-104s were transported to Edwards AFB in February 1954 and test pilot Tony LeVier commenced taxying trials on February 27, 1954. A brief take-off was achieved during further taxi runs the following day.

F-104A-10-LO STARFIGHTER (56-0756)

Edwards AFB, 1963. The first of three NF-104As converted with a rocket booster for astronaut training. 56-0756 would set an unofficial world altitude record by achieving 120,800ft on December 6, 1963. Before that, the aircraft had been damaged when a rocket oxidizer vessel exploded – removing parts of the tail section. It happened again in 1971 and this time the aircraft was damaged beyond repair, marking the end of the NF-104 programme. 56-0756 is in part preserved because portions of it were used to create the 56-0760 airframe which sits on a pole outside of the Air Force Flight Test Center at Edwards AFB.

F-104A-10-LO STARFIGHTER (56-0757)

Naval Weapons Center China Lake, 1961. This aircraft was assigned to the NWC for Navy suitability tests – the Navy having lacked a high-speed interceptor since the F3H Demon had proven too slow for the role. The Navy F-104 had its ventral fin removed, thereby distinguishing it from other F-104s. The aircraft crashed during AIM-9 Sidewinder tests on April 7, 1961. The pilot died on April 28 from the injuries he sustained.

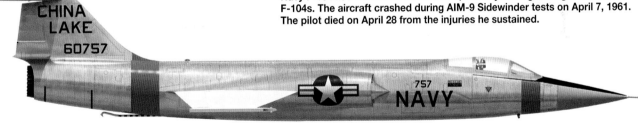

F-104C-5-LO STARFIGHTER (63-0891)

479th Tactical Fighter Wing, 1959. The 50s and 60s was a colourful era for the USAF and this CO bird of the 479th TFW certainly proves that point. The four colours on the nose, tiptank and intake cone represent the four attached units: the 434th, 435th, 436th and 476th Tactical Fighter Squadrons. This aircraft is today preserved at the Arizona ANG base at Phoenix airport.

Lockheed F-104 Starfighter

The first official flight was on March 4. It lasted 20 minutes and the only difficulty LeVier encountered was an inability to retract the undercarriage. An attempt to correct this on the day failed and the problem was later traced to a lack of hydraulic pressure. Four months after testing began, in July 1954, the first XF-104 prototype's engine was replaced with a Wright J65-W-7 – which included an afterburner. The USAF was satisfied with the progress made up to this point and therefore placed an order for 17

YF-104A pre-production aircraft. The second prototype flew for the first time on October 5, 1954.

LeVier faced a dangerous situation during cannon firing trials in the first prototype on December 17. A shell exploded in the breech, which caused fragments of the ammo and the cannon itself to pierce a fuel cell, flooding the gun bay and the engine with jet fuel. The pilot cut the engine and managed to bring the aircraft in for a successful dead stick landing at Edwards AFB.

With repairs having been made, the first prototype managed to hit Mach 1.79 at 60,000ft – an incredible feat for the still-underpowered aircraft. The second prototype was destroyed on April 15, 1955, during cannon firing trials. Vibrations from the cannon at 40,000ft blew off the ejection seat door, causing test pilot Herman 'Fish' Salmon's pressure suit to inflate. Having lost visibility, Salmon assumed this was the same problem previously encountered by LeVier and exited

F-104C-5-LO STARFIGHTER (56-0886) ▽

479th Tactical Fighter Squadron, 436th Tactical Fighter Squadron, 1965. The 479th TFW, operating the F-104C, was among the first units to be deployed in Vietnam. Later the aircraft would sport the SEA camo scheme and today is preserved at Holloman AFB.

F-104C-10-LO STARFIGHTER (57-0928) ▽

479th Tactical Fighter Wing, 435th Tactical Fighter Squadron, 1967. Upon returning from Vietnam, this aircraft was transferred to the Puerto Rico ANG and was destroyed by Puerto Rican separatists on January 11, 1981.

the aircraft using the downwards-firing C-1 ejection seat. However, later investigation revealed that if Salmon had stuck with the aircraft, descended a little and waited for his suit to deflate, the aircraft could have been saved. Apparently there were doubts about Salmon's account of what happened so he agreed to be interrogated under the influence of a 'truth drug' to set the record straight.

The surviving XF-104 was eventually destroyed on July 11, 1957, when flutter tore the tail off. Pilot William M 'Bill' Park was able to safely eject. Meanwhile, the first YF-104A had made its flight debut – with Salmon at the

controls – on February 17, 1956. The YF-104A's fuselage was extended by 1.68m compared to that of the XF-104, allowing it to accommodate the J79-GE-3A engine (9600lb-ft thrust or 14,800lb-ft with afterburner) and additional fuel tanks. To compensate, the fin was enlarged too and the wingspan was increased. The nosewheel was altered to retract forwards, rather than backwards (to allow better clearance for the downwards-firing ejection system), and the air intakes on either side of the aircraft were fitted with adjustable shock cones and internal bleed slot.

Just 11 days after the first YF-104A flight, the same aircraft achieved Mach 2

in level flight – the first jet-engined aircraft ever to do so. The USAF placed its first full production order for the aircraft on March 2, 1956, going so far as to specify four versions – the F-104A day fighter for USAF Air Defense Command, the F-104B two-seat trainer for the F-104A, the F-104C fighter-bomber for USAF Tactical Air Command and the F-104D two-seat trainer for the F-104C.

Later that year, Lockheed received a separate contract for a dedicated reconnaissance variant – the RF-104A – known informally as the 'Stargazer'. This contract would soon be cancelled, however, as the USAF concentrated on the RF-101 for its reconnaissance needs.

Lockheed F-104 Starfighter

The YF-104B first flew on January 16, 1957. It was similar to the F-104A in most respects, with the second cockpit being created using the space where the Vulcan cannon was otherwise intended to go. Other changes included a larger canopy, a backwards retracting nosewheel, extended tailfin, and larger rudder (to compensate for aerodynamic interference caused by the canopy extension).

The standard F-104A, which formally entered USAF service in February 1958, had a reinforced airframe compared to the pre-production aircraft, a J79-GE-3B engine with increased reliability,

a ribbon-style brake parachute, no cannon (since there were still problems with the Vulcan at this time), a Sidewinder on each wingtip, the option to fit underwing drop tanks, and wing leading edges so sharp they had to be covered with felt strips during maintenance to protect ground crews.

Between February and December 1958, 153 F-104As were delivered to the USAF – with some of the 17 YF-104As eventually produced being brought up to F-104A standard and also put into service. A total of 26 F-104Bs were built. While this was going on, Starfighters

broke several performance records: USAF Major Howard C 'Scrappy' Johnson broke the world altitude record at 91,249ft in a YF-104A on May 7, 1958; USAF Captain Walter Irwin set a world speed record by averaging 1404.19mph over a 9.3 by 15.5 mile circuit on May 16 and in December an F-104A flown from the Point Mugu naval air station in California broke a series of climb rate records.

Unfortunately, the early J79 engine was unreliable and 21 pilots lost their lives testing the F-104. The downwards-firing ejection seat was useless when accidents and failures occurred at low

F-104C-10-LO STARFIGHTER (57-0920) ▽

156th Tactical Fighter Group, 198th Tactical Fighter Squadron, Puerto Rico ANG, 1971. The 198th TFS was the last unit in the USAF to operate the F-104. It finally traded its F-104s for A-7D Corsair IIs in 1975. This aircraft is preserved at the South Carolina ANG base at McEntyre AFB.

level. After just a few months in service the F-104A was grounded due to concerns about its mechanical issues and poor handling in flight. In addition, the afterburner could not be regulated so pilots had a choice of flying at Mach 1 without afterburner or Mach 2.2 with afterburner and nothing in between.

The first F-104C fighter-bomber variant flew on July 24, 1958, and went into production later in the year. Similar to the F-104A, the main differences were the option to fit a fixed inflight refuelling probe, a centreline pylon for carrying nuclear stores, the improved J79-GE-7A engine and the upwards-firing C-2 ejection seat.

Deliveries of 77 F-104Cs took place between late 1958 and late 1959. A new world altitude record of 103,389ft was set in an F-104C on December 14, 1959.

The F-104D included most of the F-104C's features but the canopy now incorporated a fixed centre section between the front and rear seats – so that both positions could have an upwards-firing ejection seat. The first of 21 F-104Ds made its flight debut on October 31, 1958.

A total of just 294 Starfighters were built for the USAF, excluding the two prototypes.

US SERVICE

Despite its outstanding performance on paper, the USAF was less than impressed with the F-104 in practical terms. The J79 engine suffered an ongoing series of failures and the type's performance made it demanding to fly and unforgiving of errors. The downward-firing ejection system reduced survivability in the event of an emergency and 49 F-104s were lost in accidents up to 1961.

The F-104 was equally weak as a weapons system. Its range was limited, its payload capacity was small and its avionics were inadequate. Every surviving F-104A and B had been transferred to ANG units by late 1960, although some would be returned to USAF ADC service during moments of crisis at various times prior to 1969. A few ended up in foreign service and some YF-104As were converted into

▼ F-104C-5-LO STARFIGHTER (56-0890)

86th Air Division, 151st Fighter Interceptor Squadron, Tennessee ANG, 1961. A few USAF ANG units would operate F-104s and the 151st was one of them, flying the aircraft from 1960 to 1963. This aircraft is currently preserved at McGhee-Tyson Airport, Tennessee, sporting the serial FG-880.

Lockheed F-104 Starfighter

47773
4347

FG-773

F-104J STARFIGHTER (76-8685) ▼

203rd Sqn, Japanese Air Self-Defence Force, 1982. This aircraft was built by Mitsubishi in 1967 and entered service the same year. It would remain in service until 1984 when the 203rd Sqn replaced their F-104Js with F-15J Eagles. The whereabouts of this aircraft is uncertain as the last reported sighting was in 1997.

685

F-104A-15-LO STARFIGHTER (56-0788) ▼

9th Squadron, Royal Jordanian Air Force, 1969. This aircraft was delivered to the ROCAF before being transferred to the RJAF. It was then moved on to the PAF in December 1971.

91.

F-104G STARFIGHTER (64-17773)

3rd Tactical Fighter Squadron, 427th Tactical Fighter Squadron, Republic of China Air Force, 1967. This aircraft was built by Canadair and delivered to the Republic of China Air Force in 1965. It was being piloted by Captain Shih-Lin Hu on January 13, 1967, when he shot down a Chinese-made MiG-19 (Shenyang J-6) with an AIM-9B Sidewinder. The aircraft would later crash on April 29, 1971.

Lockheed F-104 Starfighter

QF-104A target drones complete with bright orange paintwork, starting as early as 1960.

Three F-104As were modified to become NF-104As for astronaut qualification during the early 60s. Each had its military equipment stripped out before being fitted with a new metal nose featuring hydrogen peroxide reaction thrusters for control at high altitude; new wings providing a span increase to 25.9ft with two reaction thrusters in each wingtip; new avionics and radios; a secondary hydrogen peroxide fuel system; a

bigger tailfin from the TF-104G; longer intake cones; the improved J79-GE-3B engine and finally a Rocketdyne LR121/AR-2-NA-1 liquid fuel rocket motor mounted at the bottom of the tailfin, providing 6000lb-ft of thrust.

One of the NF-104As reached a record-breaking 118,860ft on November 15, 1963, and the record was broken again on December 6, 1963, at 120,800ft. One was lost on December 10 but the two survivors continued to be used into the 1970s – finally being retired in December 1971.

The F-104C proved to be more

useful and more reliable than the F-104A and 28 were sent to the South East Asian Theatre in April 1965. From Da Nang Air Base in South Vietnam, they flew combat air patrols to defend EC-121 Warning Star radar aircraft. Despite having a strong incentive to attempt an attack on the EC-121s, the North Vietnamese never did and the F-104Cs saw no air-to-air action. They did see action in the ground-attack role against targets in South Vietnam however.

By Christmas 1965, the F-104Cs had been replaced by the F-4

Phantom. Eight returned in June 1966 to provide top cover during F-105F Wild Weasel missions but two were shot down by SAMs in this role, and their pilots killed, on August 1, 1966. The F-104s went back to close-support missions but three were lost – on September 1, October 2 and October 20, 1966, with their pilots being killed or captured. After a brief return to EC-121 defence, the surviving Starfighters were returned to the US in July 1967. In the process, the F-104 was phased out of front-line USAF service and saw out its days with ANG units before a final phase-out during the mid-1970s.

NASA received the seventh YF-104A in August 1956 and the aircraft would remain in service as an 'F-104N' – the N standing for NASA – up to 1975. Three further aircraft, all F-104Gs (see below), joined the fleet in 1963 and all four were used for testing and as chase aircraft. One was lost on June 8, 1966, when it was operating as a chase aircraft during a photoshoot for the North American XB-70 Valkyrie supersonic bomber prototype. Caught in a vortex behind the huge aircraft, the F-104N flown by test pilot Joe Walker was flipped over and crashed into one of the XB-70's fins. Walker was killed, as was XB-70 co-pilot Major Carl Cross. The XB-70's pilot, Alvin White, survived.

Another two F-104s were later obtained by NASA, along with two ex-West German TF-104Gs in 1975 – for a total of eight F-104Ns. One single-seat and one two-seat F-104N were still being operated by NASA into the 90s.

FOREIGN PRODUCTION AND SERVICE

During the mid-1950s, NATO forces in Europe (with the exceptions of Britain and France) were looking to acquire a new multi-role supersonic fighter capable of carrying a US-made tactical nuclear weapon.

In particular, West Germany wanted to replace its F-84 Thunderstreaks, F-86 Sabres and naval Hawker Seahawks – ideally with a single aircraft. Other nations, including the Netherlands,

▼ F-104A-25-LO STARFIGHTER (56-0877)

9th Squadron, Pakistan Air Force, 1965. This aircraft served with the USAF from 1958 to 1960 before being delivered to the Pakistan Air Force in late 1960. It served during the Indo-Pakistani war but was written off on September 7, 1965. Some sources claim it was a mid-air collision, others that it was shot down by an Indian Dassault Mystére.

▼ RF-104G-LO STARFIGHTER (62-12237)

331 Squadron, Royal Norwegian Air Force, 1969. This aircraft was delivered to Norway as a part of the MAP in 1963. Its service period was cut short when it crashed into Skotstind Mountain on February 10, 1971, due to poor weather conditions. The pilot, Løytn Richard Herbert Nyen, was killed.

F-104G STARFIGHTER (C/N 8053) ▼

306 Sqn, Royal Netherlands Air Force, 1966. This Fokker-built Starfighter entered service with the RNAF in 1963 and would remain in service until 1984. Today it is on display at Air Operations Control Station Nieuw-Milligen.

Belgium, Italy, Denmark, Greece, Norway, Spain and Turkey, as well as Canada and Japan, were paying close attention as West Germany assessed a wide field of competitors. It was perceived that whichever aircraft was chosen might well be purchased by the others too. Such were the financial stakes, the contest was dubbed the 'sale of the century'.

From the US, Lockheed offered the F-104, Grumman the F11F-1F Super Tiger, Convair the F-102 Delta Dagger, Republic the F-105 Thunderchief, Vought the F8U Crusader, North American the F-100J (a paper project for an improved Super Sabre) and Northrop the N-156 (another unbuilt project). From the UK, the English Electric Lightning and

Saunders-Roe SR.177 were offered; and from France came the Dassault Mirage III and Sud SO.9050 Trident III. Saab also threw its hat into the ring with the J35 Draken.

The F-104 variant offered by Lockheed was dubbed the F-104G. It was essentially an F-104C with a strengthened fuselage and wings, an increased payload capacity of 4000lb, a new radar, the bigger tailfin of the F-104B/D two-seaters, improved brakes with anti-skid system, increased internal fuel capacity, improved flight control system, the J79-GE-11A engine with 15,800lb-ft of thrust and upwards firing C-2 ejection seat (F-104s would later be retrofitted with British Martin-Baker Mk.7 zero-zero ejection seats). The M61A1

Vulcan cannon was also installed on the F-104G. The goal of these upgrades was to transform the F-104 from (largely) dedicated day fighter to true all-weather multi-role combat machine.

Much to the consternation of the other 'players', and amid allegations of bribery and other skulduggery, the Germans selected the F-104G as the winner on October 24, 1958, with the official declaration being made on November 6. The other competitors were particularly surprised at this outcome because the F-104's poor accident record was already common knowledge by this point and it was already clear that the USAF was getting cold feet about the type.

However, a key aspect of the F-104G project was the potential for German

▼ F-104G STARFIGHTER (C/N 9029)

350 Sqn, Belgian Air Force, 1972. This aircraft was built by Sociétés Anonyme Belge de Constructions Aéronautiques (SABCA) in Belgium and would serve with the Belgian Air Force from 1963 to 1979. It is currently on display at the Royal Museum of the Armed Forces and Military History, Brussels.

companies to build the F-104G in West Germany. It was an opportunity to create jobs and inject cash into the Germany economy as well as providing German workers with valuable new skills. Technology transfer was part of the deal and it was a chance to reinvigorate the German aviation industry.

A consortium of companies led by Messerschmitt reached a licensing agreement to built 210 F-104Gs on March 18, 1959. Lockheed next signed a deal with Canadian company Canadair on July 24, 1959, to allow licence production of the fighter as the CF-104 for Royal Canadian Air Force units in Europe. The Netherlands signed a licensing agreement for production by Fokker on April 20, 1960, and Belgium signed a

similar deal, with Société Anonyme de Constructions Aéronautiques (SABCA) doing the construction, on June 20 that year. In November, it was announced that Mitsubishi Heavy Industries in Japan would also build its own F-104 variant – the F-104J – which would be based on the F-104G. Finally, Italy also signed on for licence production via Fiat on March 20, 1961.

To get the ball rolling, West Germany bought a batch of 30 two-seat F-104F trainers from Lockheed in late 1959. These were effectively F-104Ds but with the J79-GE-11A engine and simpler avionics. From 1968 to 1972, five working groups in Germany produced a grand total of 1127 F-104Gs, 220 TF-104G trainers and 189 RF-104Gs. The German

Air Force and Navy received 749 RF/F-104Gs and 137 TF-104Gs – although not all of these came from the German production lines. As many had predicted, these aircraft suffered an apparently high accident rate – 298 of the German aircraft were written off and 116 pilots were killed. The argument has subsequently been made that, given the large number of aircraft in service, and the length of time that they served, this accident rate was actually no worse than that suffered by other types of the period.

Canadair made 200 CF-104s as well as a further 140 F-104Gs for MAP (NATO's Mutual Defence Assistance Program) and components for yet another 66 F-104Gs that were delivered to and assembled by Lockheed for the

TF-104G-LO STARFIGHTER (63-12684) ▽

Eskadrille 726, Royal Danish Air Force, 1968. This Lockheed-built TF-104 went directly to the Royal Danish Air Force as part of MAP. It arrived at Aalborg AB in the summer of 1965 and would remain in RDAF service until March 1987. At this point it was shipped off to continued service with the Republic of China Air Force.

F-104G-CA STARFIGHTER (64-17754) ▽

Eskadrille 726, Royal Danish Air Force, 1979. This aircraft was built by Canadair in early 1965 and shipped to Denmark immediately after completion as a part of the Mutual Defence Assistance Program (MAP). The aircraft would remain in RDAF service until early 1987, when it was shipped to Taiwan.

F-104G STARFIGHTER (C/N 8044) ▽

agdgeschwader 71 'Richthofen', 1965. This Fokker-built F-104G served with the Luftwaffe from July 1963 to 1988 when it was scrapped.

12684

17754

F-104G STARFIGHTER (C/N 8100) ▽

Jagdgeschwader 71 'Richthofen', 1971. Another Fokker-built F-104G that served exclusively with the Luftwaffe. The aircraft was withdrawn from use in December 1978 only to be rebuilt as a F-104CCV fly-by-wire research aircraft – being fitted with an additional horizontal stabilizer behind the cockpit. The aircraft remains intact and can be seen at the Wehrtechnische Studiensammlung, Koblenz, Germany.

TF-104G STARFIGHTER (62-12278) ▽

104th Sqn, Spanish Air Force, 1968. This Lockheed-built two-seater entered service with the Spanish Air Force in 1965. It served with the 161st and the 104th Sqn until June 1, 1972, when it was transferred to the Hellenic Air Force. It was written off in 1993 and wound up derelict at Tatoi AB.

German Air Force. A total of 38 CF-104D trainers were bought from Lockheed.

The CF-104 was similar to the F-104G but powered by a J79-OEL-7 turbojet – which was a J79-GE-7A built by Canadian company Orenda under licence. CF-104s were not originally fitted with the Vulcan cannon nor gunsights but these were retrofitted to most examples during the early 1970s. Most of Canada's CF-104s were operated exclusively in Europe and their replacement with CF-18s commenced in 1983, being completed in 1986. Some of the surviving aircraft were transferred to Turkey, Denmark and Norway.

In Belgium, SABCA built 100 F-104Gs for the Belgian Air Force, with Lockheed supplying 12 TF-104G trainers. All surviving Belgian F-104s were replaced with General Dynamics F-16As and Bs in the early 1980s. The Netherlands operated 120 RF/F-104Gs and 19 TF-104G trainers, replacing them with F-16As and Bs in 1984.

Norway received 19 F-104Gs and two TF-104Gs in 1963. Eighteen CF-104s

▼ F-104G STARFIGHTER (C/N 7033)

Jagdbombergeschwader 34 'Allgäu', 1984. This aircraft was built by Messerschmitt in Germany in 1963 and would serve in the Luftwaffe until 1988. It served with the JaboG 34 in 1984 sporting this unusual Norm 83 paint scheme. Today the aircraft is on display at the Szolnok Aviation Museum in Hungary.

and four CF-104Ds were then received in 1973. These were replaced with F-16As and Bs in 1982-83, with surviving F-104s going to Turkey.

The latter's usage of the F-104 had begun in May 1963 when it took receipt of its first F-104G – with another 31 following along with four TF-104Gs. Turkey then procured 40 new F-104S aircraft from

Italy and starting in 1980 began to acquire more and more F-104s from other nations that were retiring them. In total, Turkey operated more than 400 F-104s – making Turkey the second largest operator of the type after Germany. The Starfighter continued in Turkish service up to 1996 – at which point it was finally replaced by F-16Cs and Ds.

Denmark started receiving its F-104Gs in November 1964 – receiving 25 plus four TF-104Gs. During 1972-73, the nation also received 15 CF-105s and seven CF-104Ds from Canada. The F-104 left Danish service officially on April 30, 1986, with the type being rather unsurprisingly replaced with F-16As and Bs.

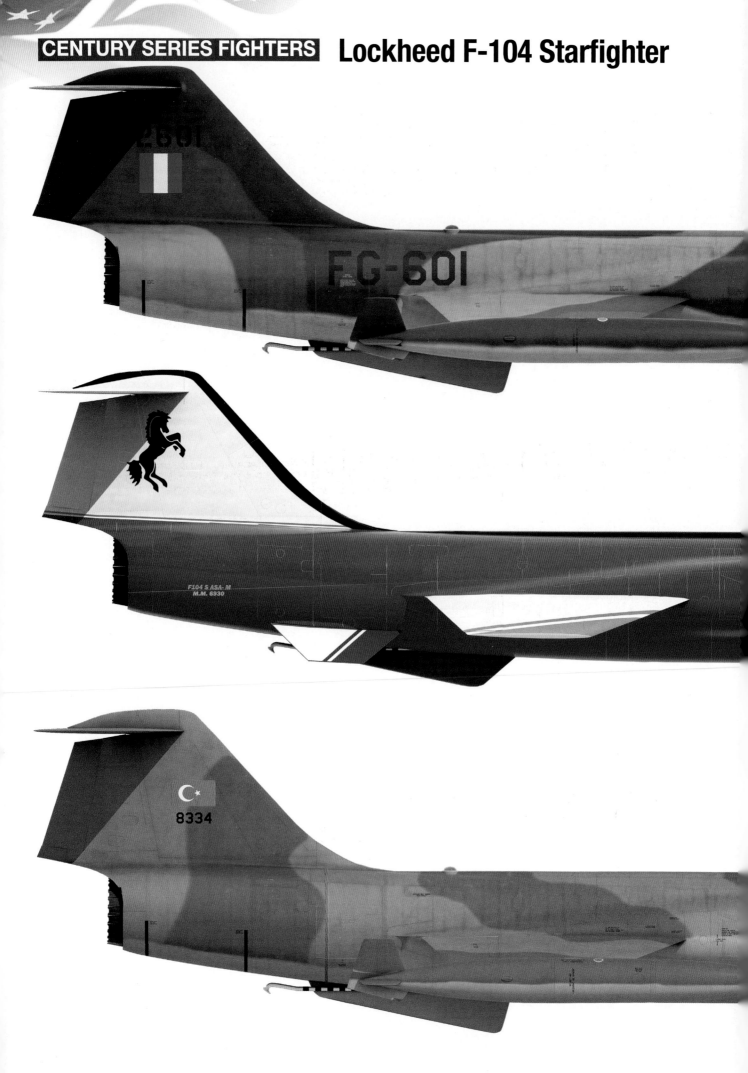

▼ F-104G STARFIGHTER (61-2061)

335 Sqn, Hellenic Air Force, 1979. A Lockheed-built Starfighter that started its life in the USAF 4443ʳᵈ CCTS (Combat Crew Training Squadron), this aircraft then went on to join the Hellenic Air Force under MAP. It served in Greece from 1969 to the early 90s when it was written off, eventually ending up as a hulk at the end of the runway at Larissa AB.

▼ F-104S ASA-M STARFIGHTER (C/N 6930)

9ᵗʰ Stormo, 10ᵗʰ Gruppo, Italian Air Force, 2003. This was the last F-104 to operate in the Italian Air Force and was unveiled in this flashy red paint scheme on September 19, 2003, to mark the end of a service career spanning five decades.

▼ F-104G STARFIGHTER (C/N 8334)

181 Filo, Turkish Air Force, 1993. This aircraft was built by Fokker in Holland and served with the Luftwaffe until 1987, when it was transferred to the Turkish Air Force.

Lockheed F-104 Starfighter

Starting in 1965, Spain received 18 F-104Gs and three TF-104G trainers. However, Spain then bought the F-4C in 1972 and no longer required its 21 F-104s. These were handed back to the US and eventually ended up serving with Greece and Turkey.

Greece initially received 45 F-104Gs and six TF-104Gs, commencing in 1964. Thirty-five of them were built by Canadair, with the remaining 10 plus the trainers supplied by Lockheed. In 1971, Greece acquired three more TF-104Gs from West Germany, and the following year it picked up another nine F-104Gs and one TF-104G from Spain. The Hellenic Air Force next received another 10 F-104Gs from the Netherlands in 1982, followed by 38 F-104Gs, 22 RF-104Gs and 20 TF-104Gs from West Germany from

1981 to 1988. Some of these additional aircraft were stripped for spares while others went into service. The last Greek Starfighters were eventually phased out during the early 1990s.

Italy received 125 RF/F-104Gs plus 28 TF-104Gs in 1963 but from 1969 these were supplemented by the first of 165 F-104S aircraft built by Fiat. The S stood for 'Sparrow', because these Starfighters included an onboard electronics suite which enabled them to operate the AIM-7 Sparrow missile. The equipment was installed in the cannon bay, which meant that the F-104S had to rely solely on its missile armament. Other changes for the S included the J79-GE-19 engine, slightly enlarged air intakes and steel inlet guide vanes, two

extra keel fins for improved longitudinal stability, and an increase in the number of external stores hardpoints to nine.

With these changes the F-104S could hit Mach 2.2. Thanks to these improvements, Italy was able to keep its advanced F-104 fleet in service longer than anyone else – the last examples finally being retired in 2004.

The Japanese Air Self-Defence Force procured 210 F-104Js and 20 two-seat F-104DJs from Mitsubishi. The company received three F-104s as pattern aircraft and constructed 29 F-104Js and all of the F-104DJs from kits before building the other aircraft from locally manufactured components. The first F-104J made its flight debut on June 30, 1961.

CF-104 STARFIGHTER (104838) ▽

439 Sqn, Royal Canadian Air Force, 1977. The RCAF has a long tradition of colourful special paint schemes – its tiger-striped Starfighters being particularly well known. This aircraft participated in the Tiger Meet exercise in 1977 sporting this great-looking scheme. The aircraft was struck off charge in 1978.

The F-104J was based on the F-104G/TF-104G but modified primarily for the air-to-air role. It was powered by a J79-IHI-11A engine – a J79-GE-11A licence-built by Ishikawajima-Harima Heavy Industries (IHI) – and armed with Sidewinders. Japan's F-104Js were eventually retired in the mid-1980s and replaced with McDonnell F-15J Eagles. During the 1990s, a handful would end up as QF-104J target drones.

From 1960 to 1961, Taiwan received 24 former F-104As and five F-104Bs from the US; it then acquired another 46 F-104Gs and eight TF-104Gs from Lockheed between 1964 and 1969. Six former American ANG F-104Ds joined the fleet in 1975 and eight years later Taiwan took on 38 F-104Gs and 26 TF-104Gs from West Germany. Next, in 1987, it took possession of 22 F-104Js and five F-104DJs from Japan plus 15 F-104Gs

and three TF-104Gs from Denmark. The last Taiwanese-operated F-104s were retired at the end of the 1990s.

Pakistan's Starfighters, perhaps, saw more action than those of any other nation. The Pakistani Air Force (PAF) received 10 former USAF F-104As and two F-104Bs in 1961 and used them in combat against Indian forces during the 1965 war between those two countries – achieving (according to the PAF) a respectable ratio of four kills to two losses. The two losses were made up when Pakistan acquired two F-104As from Taiwan's complement.

The US government put Pakistan under embargo in 1965, which resulted in the country's F-104 fleet entering a period of decline. During the 1971 war with India, seven more Starfighters were lost. The surviving F-104s were replaced with French Dassault Mirage 5s in the mid-1970s.

During the late 1960s, Jordan acquired 18 former USAF F-104As and six F-104Bs. The first examples were delivered just in time to for the Six-Day War of June 5-10, 1967. However, since the Royal Jordanian Air Force's pilots had not yet received sufficient training on the type to fly it in combat, the aircraft were transferred to Turkey – where they remained safe even as most of the rest of Jordan's air force was destroyed on the ground. The balance of the Jordanian tranche was delivered after the war and these were supplemented by further aircraft from Taiwan's stock. Jordan's F-104s then took part in the 1971 Indo-Pakistan War, where they suffered a number of losses to the Indian Air Force.

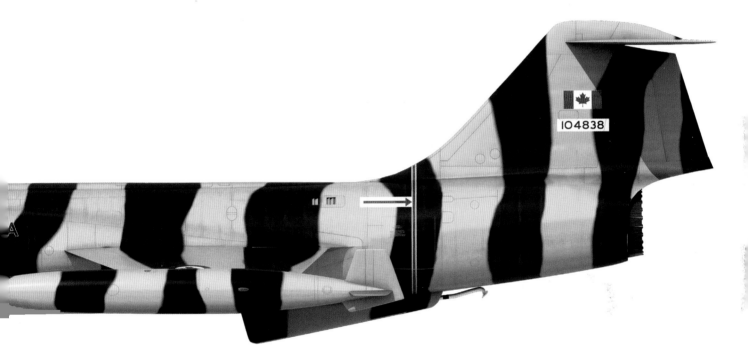

▼ F-104N STARFIGHTER (56-0790)

NASA, 1971. This aircraft started its life as a F-104A-20-LO and went into service as a test plane for NACA, NASA, Lockheed and ARDC. Among its many missions was flying as a chase plane in the X-15 programme. The aircraft was converted to F-104G standard in late 1959, only to be subsequently redesignated F-104N. The aircraft in its depicted configuration flew with NASA from 1970 to 1980 sporting the civil registration N820NA. The aircraft is now parked outside Edwards AFB in the 'Century Circle' near the west gate.

REPUBLIC F-105 THUNDERCHIEF

1955-1984

Designed as a Mach 2 nuclear fighter-bomber, the F-105 Thunderchief or 'Thud' would become synonymous with hazardous strike missions over heavily defended targets during the Vietnam War.

Republic had achieved a surprising degree of success with its somewhat lacklustre F-84 Thunderjet design – not as the day fighter it was originally intended to be but as a fighter-bomber capable of carrying a nuclear payload. Thousands of F-84s were built, starting with the first prototype in 1946, and as this process continued into 1951 the company's designers led by Alexander Kartveli commenced work on a successor.

Despite there being no formal requirement for this new aircraft from the USAF, Republic had enough confidence in Kartveli to back the project with its own funds. The concept was known as Advanced Project 63 Fighter Bomber Experimental or 'AP-63FBX'. Rather than design a pure fighter and have it retroactively equipped for strike missions, Republic wanted to create a dedicated fighter-bomber from the start.

A total of 108 different arrangements were reputedly examined before the design team picked configuration AP-63-31 for further development. The aircraft was specifically tailored for low-altitude performance – with a big engine, small wings, low drag, state-of-the-art avionics and the ability to carry a heavy payload, particularly a nuclear payload. Less emphasis was placed on traditional 'fighter features' such as manoeuvrability and high rate of climb, although the aircraft would be able to carry air-to-air missiles and four T-130 machine guns with which to defend itself.

The resulting design was powered by a single Allison J71 turbojet and initially looked something like an elongated F-84F with enough room to carry a single nuclear bomb.

The USAF received Republic's proposal, submitted in April 1952, with enthusiasm and an order was placed for 199 aircraft under the designation F-105A that September. Delivery of the first example was due in 1955

F-105B-5-RE THUNDERCHIEF (54-0107) ▽

Air Research and Development Command, 1959. This was one of the earliest Thunderchiefs and like many pre-production aircraft it was used primarily for tests – in this case cold weather testing. It set a new speed record when Captain Billy White flew it from Eielson AFB, Alaska, to Eglin AFB, Florida, in five hours 27 minutes on January 22, 1959. It was later withdrawn from use and preserved, recently being restored and put on display at the Hickory Aviation Museum, North Carolina.

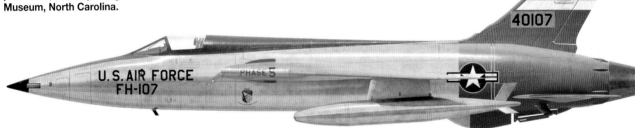

F-105B-15-RE THUNDERCHIEF (57-5787) ▽

USAF demonstration team Thunderbirds, 1964. The Thunderbirds were equipped with the F-100C Super Sabre up to the 1964 season, when they received the far larger F-105 Thunderchief. The Thunderchief's career with the Thunderbirds was short, with only six shows flown before the team reverted back to the F-100 (this time the D model). The cause for this early retirement was a catastrophic structural failure of one of the team's Thunderchiefs. The aircraft pictured here would go on to serve with the New Jersey ANG until its retirement in December 1980.

▽ F-105D-5-RE THUNDERCHIEF (58-1158)

4th Tactical Fighter Squadron, 335th Tactical Fighter Wing, 1962. The 335th TFS flew F-105s from as early as 1959 and the unit markings on the D model were very similar those applied to the F-105B model that preceded it, although these were worn for only a short time. 58-1158 suffered engine failure during take-off from Korat AB, Thailand, on April 15, 1966, and crashed on the unpaved overrun. Pilot Captain John A McCurdy was killed.

Republic F-105 Thunderchief

but within six months the order had been cut back to 37 fighter-bombers and nine examples of a proposed reconnaissance version. A mock-up was inspected in October 1953 but two months later Republic was informed that the whole development programme was being cancelled.

The Korean War had ended and the USAF's priorities had shifted. Meanwhile, Republic continued to work on the F-105's design, changing

it substantially. The nose intake was replaced with new side intakes, the four machine guns were replaced with a single General Electric T-171D 20mm rotary cannon and the whole aircraft ballooned in size.

For a time it appeared as though Republic's new fighter was dead in the water but finally, on June 28, 1954, the company received a fresh contract for 15 aircraft under Weapon System 306A. These included two YF-105As,

four YF-105Bs, six F-105Bs and three RF-105B reconnaissance aircraft.

The YF-104A prototypes would be powered by Pratt & Whitney's J57 engine while the YF-105Bs would receive the J71 itself but would lack radar and other military equipment. The F-105B represented the first full production model and was equipped with AN/APN-105 navigation radar.

Work progressed but in September 1954 the company was told that only

F-105D-10-RE THUNDERCHIEF (60-0482) ▽

36th Tactical Fighter Wing, 23rd Tactical Fighter Squadron, 1965. 60-0482 would be sent to Vietnam where it flew with the 388th TFW and had the name 'Iron Butterfly'. The aircraft was severely battle damaged in September 1966 but parts of it were salvaged and survived in the form of a composite aircraft – still with the 60-0482 serial number. Today the aircraft is on display at Valiant Air Command museum, Titusville, Florida.

three aircraft would be required. This was revised to six in October and back up to 15 in February 1955. The USAF had by now realised that the F-105 was lacking three key features: inflight refuelling capability, an advanced fire control system and perhaps most importantly, speed.

As a result, in April 1955, the J71 was switched for the Pratt & Whitney J75-P-3 (the J57's big brother), which provided 23,500lb of thrust compared to the J71's 14,000lb-ft.

Republic chief experimental test pilot Russell Morgan 'Rusty' Roth took the first YF-105A up for its initial flight on October 22, 1955, and it went supersonic later that day. Further testing would show that even with the J57 it was capable of Mach 1.2. However, Roth was forced to make an emergency landing at Edwards AFB on December 16, 1955, after the YF-105A's right main landing gear assembly was torn off during high-speed flight. Its up-lock mechanism had failed, causing it to drop out its well and into the airsteam. The aircraft suffered heavy damage, which Republic deemed too costly to repair, and Roth was injured.

The second YF-105A, with strengthened up-locks on its landing gear, made its flight debut on January 28, 1956 – with a recovered Roth at the controls. The USAF ordered five two-seat trainers under the designation F-105C in April 1956 and Republic commenced work on a life-size engineering mock-up.

The first YF-105B flew on May 26, 1956, and was the first J75-powered F-105. It also had new forward-swept intakes with adjustable ramps and a curved 'wasp-waist' fuselage to take advantage of the newly discovered 'area-rule' effect when going supersonic (the YF-104As had both been 'slab-sided'). Test pilot Lindell Eugene 'Lin' Hendrix was in the air for about an hour but when he came in to land the nosewheel failed to extend.

▼ F-105D-5-RE THUNDERCHIEF (59-1750)

4th Tactical Fighter Squadron, 335th Tactical Fighter Wing, 1965. During their early involvement in the Vietnam War, Thunderchiefs would be left in this natural metal finish. Often, as was the case with this aircraft, there would be no unit identifying markings. As the war progressed however, the SEA camouflage paint scheme became standard. This was the case for 59-1750 which served in Vietnam from 1965 until December 14, 1967, when it was shot down by ground fire near Hung Yen. The pilot, Major James Sehorn, survived and became a POW at the infamous 'Hanoi Hilton'.

Republic F-105 Thunderchief

The result was another crash-landing, but the aircraft suffered only minor damage and Hendrix was uninjured. However, as it was being removed from the runway at Edwards AFB, the crane operator accidentally dropped it – causing much more serious damage – and it was written off. The RF-105B reconnaissance variant was cancelled in July 1956, although the three prototypes were still eventually completed without armament or photographic gear. They would be used for trials under the designation JF-105B.

The second YF-105B wasn't ready until January 30, 1957, and it too crash-landed as a result of a landing gear problem caused by interference between the auxiliary air inlets and the main landing gear. This was resolved, the aircraft was repaired and testing recommenced.

By now it was clear that the changes implemented in the YF-105B had had the desired effect: where the YF-105As had managed to reach Mach 1.2, the YF-105B could top Mach 2, albeit with increased tail flutter – a problem overcome with the

10143

F-105D-5-RE THUNDERCHIEF (58-1156) ▼

388th Tactical Fighter Wing, 421st Tactical Fighter Squadron, 1966. About one in 20 F-105Ds were painted with 'reverse' camo pattern – where the tan and the light green colours were switched. The reason for this is unknown. This aircraft was even more special because it was the first MiG-killing F-105 of the Vietnam War. Major Fred Tracy shot down a MiG-17 using the aircraft's 20mm cannon on June 29, 1966. 58-1156 was itself shot down – by AAA fire – on January 21, 1967, ditching in the Gulf of Tonkin. The pilot was rescued by a US Navy helicopter.

LT. K. W. KICAFTE

introduction of enlarged tail surfaces. The F-105B would also get four-petal air brakes which fitted around the jet exhaust and the small cockpit canopy rear window that was a feature of the earliest F-105 airframes was deleted.

The first full production model F-105B joined the flight testing programme on May 14, 1957, and the two-seater F-105C was cancelled that October just as a mock-up of it was being readied for an official inspection. The F-105B was powered by a J75-P-19 with 16,100lb-ft of dry thrust or 24,500lb-ft with afterburner. It could carry 8000lb of stores in a bomb bay (such as a single Mark 28 or Mark 43 nuclear weapon – or an auxiliary tank carrying 390 US gallons of fuel) plus

another 4000lb on five external hardpoints – a centreline rack and two pylons under each wing. It was also armed with a single M61 20mm Vulcan cannon.

The FCS was an MA-8 with a K-19 gunsight, AN/APG-31 ranging radar and bomb-tossing system.

In November 1957, the USAF called for an all-weather version of the F-105 and the following year Republic made its proposal. The refined design would have a 1ft 3in longer nose to accommodate the AN/ASG-9 Thunderstick FCS (a dramatic improvement on the F-105B's MA-8, featuring a multi-mode radar with air-to-air, air-to-ground and low-level terrain-following capability), the J75-

P-19W turbojet with water-methanol injection (offering a maximum thrust of 26,500lb-ft), an easier-to-read instrument display, strengthened airframe and arrestor hook.

All 12,000lb of stores could now be carried externally and the aircraft could also carry four Sidewinders or four Bullpup air-to-surface missiles. The air force initially ordered 59 examples and commissioned work on a two-seater variant – the F-105E.

The first unit to receive the F-105B was the 335th Tactical Fighter Squadron, part of the 4th Tactical Fighter Wing, in August 1958, and the USAF cancelled the F-105E portion of its latest order on March 18, 1959. The first of three

▼ F-105D-20-RE THUNDERCHIEF (61-0143)

355th Tactical Fighter Wing, 354th Tactical Fighter Squadron, 1965. The 355th TFW was among the first wings to be stationed in Vietnam and the wing's aircraft flew numerous missions during the Rolling Thunder campaign. This aircraft would return to the CONUS in 1967 but crashed at the Smoky Hill ANG Range, Kansas, on November 14, 1967.

U.S. AIR FORCE
FH-143

USAF
81156

Republic F-105 Thunderchief

F-105D-1 aircraft made its flight debut on June 9, 1959, by which time the 335th was fully equipped with F-105Bs. A new world speed record of 1216mph was set by the commander of the 4th, Brigadier General Joseph Moore, on December 11, 1959.

Deliveries of the first full production F-105Ds commenced in June 1960, with the new aircraft replacing the 335th's F-105Bs, and later that year the USAF increased its order to nearly 300.

More units began to receive the aircraft during 1961 and in May of that year the F-105D was deployed abroad for the first time when examples were delivered to the 36th Tactical Fighter Wing at Bitburg in Germany. The following month, an F-105D was able to take-off carrying seven tons of bombs during testing at Eglin AFB in Florida – the heaviest bomb load ever carried by a single-engined fighter up to that point.

F-105D-20-RE THUNDERCHIEF (61-0132) ▼

388th Tactical Fighter Wing, 34th Tactical Fighter Squadron, 1968. The 'Hanoi Special' shot down one or possibly two MiG-17s on August 23, 1967, after a bombing mission. Certainly one MiG-17 was brought down by the F-105's 20mm Vulcan cannon. On May 14, 1968, the Hanoi Special collided with another F-105D (60-0428) and crashed near Korat AB, killing the pilot Major Seymour Bass.

However, that December a lab test at Wright-Patterson AFB found that cracks could appear in the F-105D airframe as a result of fatigue. All F-105Ds were immediately grounded but it was quickly determined that the cracks were not serious and Republic was able to conduct a relatively minor fix which prevented them from occurring in the first place. The whole fleet was grounded again in June 1962 after two serious accidents involving F-105Ds at Nellis AFB but again the fix was relatively easy, being traced to some electric wires and defective seals which had allowed moisture to penetrate the aircraft's systems.

Another problem was also starting to make itself known – the F-105 was not a particularly easy aircraft to fly and the 'jump' pilots were having to make from the T-33 trainer to the operational F-105D was simply too great. Cancelling the F-105E trainer had been a mistake but this error was now rectified in the F-105F.

Stretching the forward fuselage of the F-105D by 5ft created space for a 'back-seater' who received nearly a full duplicate set of controls. This meant that all of the aircraft's systems could be operated from either seat and the aircraft was fully combat capable. The aircraft's fin and rudder were enlarged to balance the altered fuselage but otherwise the design was kept as close to that of the F-105D as possible to keep costs down.

The first F-105F took its fight flight on June 11, 1963, and a total of 143 F-105Ds already on order would be built as F-105Fs instead, between 1963 and January 1965. The last F-105F to roll off the line was the last F-105 and indeed the last fighter aircraft ever built by Republic; the F-4

▲ F-105F-1-RE THUNDERCHIEF (63-8329)

355th Tactical Fighter Wing, 333rd Tactical Fighter Squadron, 1967. On December 19, 1967, this aircraft was crewed by Major Will M Dalton and Major James M Graham when it shot down a MiG-17 – the last MiG kill by a Thunderchief in the Vietnam War. It was lost on January 28, 1970, when it was hit by ground fire near Khe Ve, Vietnam. The crew, Captain Richard J Mallon and Captain Robert J Panek, ejected and survived. A helicopter sent to retrieve them was shot down by a MiG, with all six crewmen aboard being killed. Mallon and Panek were surrounded, captured and subsequently killed by the enemy.

Republic F-105 Thunderchief

F-105D-10-RE THUNDERCHIEF (60-0504) ▼

355th Tactical Fighter Wing, 357th Tactical Fighter Squadron, 1968. Lieutenant Colonel Arthur C Dennis, flying Memphis Belle II, shot down a MiG-17 on April 28, 1967, using the aircraft's 20mm Vulcan cannon. Only two days, flying the same F-105D, Dennis shot down another MiG-17. Although this kill was never confirmed, Dennis was sure enough of its authenticity to mark two red stars under the canopy to commemorate the two kills. The aircraft was retired to AMARC in June 1981 but was later restored in the colours of the Memphis Belle II and is currently on display at the USAF Museum, Wright-Patterson AFB, Ohio.

F-105F-1-RE THUNDERCHIEF (63-8268) ▼

18th Tactical Fighter Wing, 12th Tactical Fighter Squadron, 1969. This unit was stationed at Kadena AB, Korea, and operated the D, F and G model Thunderchiefs. This particular aircraft crashed on January 29, 1970, near Osan AB, South Korea, due to a mechanical failure.

F-105D-15-RE THUNDERCHIEF (61-0086)

355th Tactical Fighter Wing, 44th Tactical Fighter Squadron, 1970. This F-105D named 'Big Sal' made it out of Vietnam and would continue to fly with the USAF in the Virginia ANG (see elsewhere in this publication) until it was put into storage at AMARC on September 24, 1981. It was later put on display at the Pima Air & Space Museum, where it can still be seen to this day.

Republic F-105 Thunderchief

F-105F-1-RE THUNDERCHIEF (63-8319) ▼

355th Tactical Fighter Wing, 44th Tactical Fighter Squadron, 1970. The 'Sinister Vampire' was built as an F-105F and would eventually be upgraded to suppress enemy air defence with the unofficial designation EF-105F. In 1971 it was upgraded to F-105G standard. Here it is depicted as an F-105F while assigned to Captain Donald Kilgus who, earlier in the war, claimed a MiG-17 while flying an F-100D (see elsewhere in the publication). Although the kill wasn't officially confirmed, Kilgus still had a red star painted next to his name on the canopy rail. The aircraft survived the Vietnam War and ended its flying career at Georgia ANG. It then became a ground target at the Aberdeen Proving Ground, MD.

▼ F-105G-1-RE THUNDERCHIEF (63-8319)

The 'Sinister Vampire' was upgraded to F-105G standard in 1971 and here's how it came to look. Now named 'Tuffy', it flew missions over North Vietnam as a part of the 17th WWS, a dedicated Wild Weasel squadron. As mentioned, the aircraft survived Vietnam only to become a ground target for shooting practice.

▼ F-105G-1-RE THUNDERCHIEF (62-4440)

388th Tactical Fighter Wing, 561st Tactical Fighter Squadron in 1972. During the final years of the Vietnam War, most Thunderchiefs remaining in-theatre were Wild Weasels – like this jet. The G-model differed from the F most notably in having huge blisters on the fuselage under the wing. This aircraft is armed with AGM-45 Shrike and the AGM-78 missiles. Both were designed to home in on objects giving off radiation of a certain frequency – that produced by SAM and AAA sites radars. The 561st TFS Det. 1 flew operations out of Korat AB, Thailand in 1972, and their aircraft were adorned with the WW tailcode, giving away their primary mission as Wild Weasels. This aircraft is currently preserved at Hill AFB, Utah.

Republic F-105 Thunderchief

Phantom II had been chosen to replace it as the USAF's main fighter-bomber.

Deliveries of the F-105F to the Air Force, specifically the 4520th Combat Crew Training Wing at Nellis AFB, began on December 7. This was well timed because F-105 units were among the first to arrive in South East Asia following the Gulf of Tonkin incident on August 2, 1964. Eight F-105Ds from the 18th TFW were sent to Korat RTAFB in Thailand from Yokota AB in Japan

and missions commenced over Vietnam shortly thereafter. Most of the F-105s in-theatre would be operated from Thailand by the 355th and 388th Tactical Fighter Wings, with camouflage being added during 1965.

When equipped for a typical bombing mission over North Vietnam, an F-105D might carry five 1000lb bombs or six 750lb bombs – plus a pair of 450 gallon drop tanks. An alternative load might include canisters of napalm or 2.75in rocket pods and a quartet

of Sidewinders for air-to-air combat. The aircraft's single internal M61A1 20mm cannon was effective both for dogfighting and ground strafing.

In order to deliver its unguided munitions accurately, the F-105 had to attack at low level or in a shallow dive, putting it within range of enemy AAA. Losses rose alarmingly as a result – to the point where some consideration was given to restarting the F-105 production line to provide replacements. A total of 126 were lost

F-105B-10-RE THUNDERCHIEF (57-5776) ▼

108th Tactical Fighter Group, 141st Tactical Fighter Squadron, New Jersey ANG, 1976. New Jersey ANG were the last unit to fly the F-105B. In 1976 57-5776 was painted with this unusually colourful vertical stabiliser for the USA's bicentennial celebrations. The aircraft is currently preserved at McGuire AFB, New Jersey.

in 1966 alone, 103 of them to anti-aircraft defences.

The F-105D had not been designed for manoeuvrability and when jumped by MiG-17s or MiG-21s, particularly en route to a target, the pilot's best option was usually to drop everything, hit the deck and accelerate away. A combined total of 27 enemy fighters were downed by F-105Ds during 1966 and 1967 – most of them shot down with the M61A1. In return, 17 F-105s were shot down by North Vietnamese MiGs. A total of more than 350 F-105Ds and Fs were lost in combat over Vietnam over the course of 20,000 combat missions from 1965-1968 – nearly half of all Thuds ever built.

The complex F-105 also suffered a host of mechanical and performance issues while fighting in the extremely hot and humid conditions of South East Asia, with fuel economy being badly degraded and inflight refuelling becoming a standard part of almost every F-105D mission.

The type's hydraulics were also found to be vulnerable to ground fire. A single bullet or piece of shrapnel in the wrong place could knock out the entire flight control system, resulting in the loss of the aircraft. As a result, a number of upgrades were made in the field: armour plates were added to cover particularly vulnerable sections

▽ F-105D-20-RE THUNDERCHIEF (61-0138)

113th Tactical Fighter Group, 121st Tactical Fighter Squadron, DC ANG, 1972. In the later years of the Vietnam war, many F-105s were transferred to either the Reserve or, like this jet, ANG units. This aircraft would serve with the District of Columbia Air National Guard until it was withdrawn from service in September 1977. Today it is preserved at Boling Field, MD, marked as 'Ohio Express' 59-1771.

Republic F-105 Thunderchief

F-105D-15-RE THUNDERCHIEF (61-0086) ▼

192nd Tactical Fighter Group, 149th Tactical Fighter Squadron, 1981. 61-0086 would serve with the Virginia ANG, with the name 'Keep 'em Flying' not long before being sent AMARC – on September 4, 1981. It was later preserved and is now on display at the Pima Air & Space Museum.

▼ F-105F-1-RE THUNDERCHIEF (63-8279)

184th Tactical Fighter Training Group, 127th Tactical Fighter Training Squadron, Kansas ANG, 1973. Thuds that came home from Vietnam equipped ANG and AFRES units. The 127th TFTS had the task of training crews for the F-105 units since their Kansas ANG base was near the Smoky Hills ANG Range. 63-8279 crashed on approach to McConnell AFB, Kansas on August 28, 1976.

▼ F-105F-1-RF THUNDERCHIEF (63-8299)

116th Tactical Fighter Wing, 128th Tactical Fighter Squadron, Georgia ANG, 1983. The last flight of a USAF F-105 (not counting the AFRES) was made on May 25, 1983, when this F-105F took off for one last time. The aircraft was adorned with a few special markings for the occasion, with the crew of the squadron signing it on the fuselage below the intake. The aircraft was then moved to Aberdeen Proving Ground, MD, where it served as a target for shooting practice.

Republic F-105 Thunderchief

of the hydraulics and a third redundant system was retrofitted.

The F-105Ds also got upgraded ejection seats, better radar homing and warning antennae, improved refuelling probes, and (in some cases) new ram air scoops on the rear fuselage to improve heat management for the afterburner. This latter measure was necessary because high ambient temperatures in the region could cause an uncontrollable build-up of heat during combat operations and result in an engine fire.

The unreliability of the F-105D's AN/ARN-85 Loran radio navigation system caused problems throughout the type's career on the front line in Vietnam – so in 1969 a replacement was chosen. Thirty F-105Ds received the new AN/

F-105D-15-RE THUNDERCHIEF (61-0047) ▽

301st Tactical Fighter Wing, 457th Tactical Fighter Squadron, 1974. This F-105D was modified with the so-called Thunderstick II upgrade which aimed to improve all-weather and night bombing accuracy. The upgrade is easily recognisable as the spine of the fuselage is enlarged quite dramatically. This aircraft served with the USAFR until it crashed due to engine failure on March 21, 1978, near Roosevelt, Oklahoma.

ARN-92 Loran system – which was visible as a lengthy dorsal spine running from the canopy right back to the tail fin. These aircraft were known as Thunderstick IIs or 'T-Stick IIs', with the first modified example flying on August 9, 1969. They were, however, too late to see any combat in Vietnam and served instead with the 23rd TFW in the USA before being transferred to the ANG where they served until January 1980.

Perhaps the F-105's best-remembered role in Vietnam was as a 'Wild Weasel' aircraft. As mentioned earlier, the two-seater F-100F was originally chosen for the Wild Weasel mission as the EF-100F – being fitted with radar homing and warning electronics to detect and identify SAM and AAA sites before attacking them with gravity bombs, rockets, napalm and AGM-45 Shrike anti-radar missiles. However, the handful of Wild Weasel F-100Fs were soon replaced by EF-105Fs on the front line.

The F-105F Wild Weasel III was significantly more capable that

the EF-100F – being able to carry sophisticated jamming equipment that could prevent enemy radar from getting a solid lock during their attack. The first F-105F modified for Wild Weasel operations flew on January 15, 1966, with development work being completed in May and deployment to Southeast Asia commencing in June. During a typical Wild Weasel mission, a single F-105F would accompany two or four F-105Ds. When a SAM site was located and identified, the F-105F's jammers would confuse the enemy radar

▼ F-105F-1-RE THUNDERCHIEF (62-4413)

Air Development and Test Command, 1972. Not all Thunderchiefs were painted in SEA camo. This aircraft was painted in the ADC grey which was much more common in Air Defence Command squadrons. 62-4413 would be transferred to the ANG in 1974 and served with a few different squadrons before being sent to AMARC in November 1981. From here it ended up as a battle damage repair trainer and is currently preserved at Tinker AFB, Oklahoma.

Republic F-105 Thunderchief

▼ F-105D-31-RF THUNDERCHIEF (62-4328)

419th Tactical Fighter Wing, 466th Tactical Fighter Squadron, 1983. Among the last squadrons to operate the F-105 was the 466th, who received their Thunderchiefs from deactivated units. This late in the Thunderchief's career it wasn't unusual to see the wraparound paint scheme that is depicted here. This particular aircraft would be retired in 1984 and put on display at Arnold AFB, Texas, where it remains today.

while the attack commenced. It was a highly dangerous mission however, with five of the first 11 F-105Fs in theatre being destroyed before the end of August 1966.

A further development of the F-105F Wild Weasel was the F-105G – a modification made to 61 existing F-105F airframes. Initially given the designation EF-105F, these aircraft were fitted with the Search, Exploit and Evade Surface to Air Missile Systems system or 'SEESAMS' for short, which improved on the F-105F's radar detection capabilities, and built-in electronic countermeasures equipment. The latter were housed in long blisters that were faired into the sides of the lower fuselage and a new

air intake for their cooling mechanisms was added to the aircraft's belly.

Installing these systems internally meant the outer underwing pylons where they had previously been fitted could be used for additional missiles. However, it also meant that the F-105G's fuel tanks had to be slightly decreased in size, reducing capacity

▼ F-105D-31-RE THUNDERCHIEF (62-4301)

419th Tactical Fighter Wing, 466th Tactical Fighter Squadron, 1983. The Euro 1 paint scheme on 'My Karma' was a one-off and only applied to this one jet of the 466th TFS. The aircraft is currently preserved at the Aerospace Museum of California.

from 1160 US gallons on the F-105F to 1051 US gallons on the F-105G. The first Gs entered the war during the latter half of 1967.

The last F-105Ds were withdrawn from the theatre in October 1970 but the F-105F and F-105G Wild Weasels remained until American involvement in the conflict ended –

being gradually replaced during this time by F-4s.

In total, just 833 F-105s of all types were built and 395 of them were lost during the war – 296 F-105Ds and 38 F-105F/Gs having been destroyed by enemy action and another 61 of all types being lost due to accidents and mechanical failures.

By 1974 the only F-105s still in active operational service were F-105Fs and F-105Gs, although some F-105Ds were still flown by the Air Force Reserve. The last official USAF F-105 flight took place on May 25, 1983, with the last ever in-service F-105 flight being on February 25, 1984.

CONVAIR F-106 DELTA DART

1956-1988

Convair's F-102 interceptor fell way short of expectations when it entered service, but the company soon figured out what was holding it back and came up with the far superior F-102B design. This would enter service as the F-106 – the USAF's last pure interceptor.

It was originally intended that the F-102B would be the same as the F-102A except for its engine – which would be a Wright J67 rather than a Pratt & Whitney J57. The J67 was to be a developed licence-built version of the Bristol B.E. 10 Olympus turbojet with a projected 15,000lb-ft of thrust.

Since some development was necessary to create the J67 from the original British design, the F-102B was not expected to be ready until after testing of the F-102A had already begun. So when it became clear in November 1952 that Hughes would not have its advanced MA-1 fire control system ready in time for installation in the F-102A, it was decided that it would make its debut in the F-102B instead. The F-102A would receive the interim E-9 (later MG-10) FCS.

Difficulties with the J67 led to Convair offering two alternatives for the F-102B in October 1953: a Rolls-Royce Conway (which would eventually be capable of supplying 17,500lb-ft of thrust) or a Pratt & Whitney J75 (eventually offering 16,100lb-ft of dry thrust or 24,500lb-ft with afterburner). The Air Force opted for the latter. Convair attempted to sell a navalised carrier-based F-102B interceptor to the US Navy in June 1955 with strengthened wings, strengthened gear, folding fin tip and tailhook but to no avail.

F-106A DELTA DART (56-0467)

Illustrated as it appeared in 1959. This aircraft had a very short career in service but made a huge impact during that time. One F-106A, 56-0459, had its engine modified in an attempt to break the absolute speed record which, at the time, was in Soviet hands. However, the modifications made the engine prone to compressor stalls and it eventually became clear that the aircraft was not suitable for the task. 56-0467 was the back-up plane and was in standard configuration. The record attempt, on December 5, 1959, with Major Joseph Rogers in the cockpit, set a new absolute speed record of 1525.95mph (2455.78 km/h) over an 11-mile course. The aircraft was lost less than two years later when a tyre blew on take-off on August 14, 1961, while it was serving with the 329th FIS. The damaged aircraft was redirected to Edwards AFB, where the pilot attempted to land by keeping it on two wheels for as long as possible. With both brakes and drag chute malfunctioning, the aircraft took a long time to come to rest. While dragging its blown tyre along the runway, the aircraft caught fire and was burned beyond repair. The pilot survived even though the aircraft lacked a zero-zero ejection seat.

F-106A-125-CO DELTA DART (59-0090)

343th Fighter Group, 11th Fighter-Interceptor Squadron 'Red Bulls', 1962. The 11th FIS received their first Delta Darts in mid-1960 and would operate the 'Six' until June 1968 when the squadron was deactivated. F-106s only had the buzz number painted on their aft fuselage for a very short time, during their early years in service. Another feature only found on those early aircraft is the two-part canopy glass, divided along the aircraft's longitudinal axis in much in the same way as that of the Delta Dart's predecessor, the F-102 Delta Dagger. Later a single canopy glass was retrofitted to all F-106s. This aircraft's story is similar to that of many other F-106s. It was put in storage on January 15, 1985, and a few years later, on January 25, 1991, it was converted into a QF-106A and eventually shot down by an AIM-7M missile on March 10, 1993.

F-106A-110-CO DELTA DART (59-0034)

Bangor Air Defence Sector, 27th Fighter-Interceptor Squadron 'Fighting Falcons', 1962. The 27th FIS traded their F-102s for F-106s in 1959 and these new aircraft would carry markings very similar to those of the old ones (see elsewhere in this publication). This example was damaged in a fire on December 21, 1965, but after more than a year of repairs it made it back into service. 59-0034 would be retired on July 20, 1988, and sent to AMARC. On December 1, 1992, its conversion to QF-106 standard began and it was shot down by a Stinger missile on November 8, 1996.

Convair F-106 Delta Dart

The Air Force, however, was still interested. A contract was drawn up for the supply of 17 F-102Bs in November 1955 and this was eventually finalised and ratified on April 18, 1956. The design was by now so different from that of the F-102 that a new designation, F-106A, was applied several weeks later. A two-seat TF-106A trainer variant was then approved for development on August 3, 1956, but less than a month later this designation was altered to F-106B.

Convair was contractually obligated to have the first F-106A airborne by the end of 1956 and, with time running out, taxi tests of the first prototype commenced on December 22. The first flight had to wait until December 26 and it was not a great success, being prematurely aborted after 20 minutes due to engine problems and speed brakes which, once opened, would not close. This first F-106A (F-106A-1-CO, 56-451), flown by Convair chief test pilot Richard 'Dick' Lowe Johnson, was an aerodynamics test bed rather than a

fully-operational aircraft, since the MA-1 FCS was still far from ready. Ballast took the system's place in the nose to ensure the correct centre of gravity. In fact, Hughes had only started flight testing the system earlier that month using a modified Convair 340 airliner.

At a glance there was more than a passing similarity between the F-102A and F-106A, but despite this the two types had relatively few parts in common. The delta wing of the F-106A was developed from that of

F-106B-50-CO DELTA DART (57-2530) ▼

26th Air Division, 539th Fighter-Interceptor Squadron, 1966. This aircraft was sent to AMARC on August 25, 1987. On August 12, 1993, it was transported to AEL Inc. for drone conversion. Inevitably, on April 24, 1997, the aircraft was shot down by an AIM-120 missile.

the F-102A and had no internal fuel bladders – being effectively a tank in its own right, with air pressure being used to transfer fuel to the engine. Unfortunately, this made the F-106A particularly sensitive to battle damage since a hole in the wing would cause a corresponding loss of pressure. The fuselage was heavily revised from that of the F-102A to present a more streamlined form.

The Pratt & Whitney YJ75-P-1 turbojet was fed by variable intake ramps (which were positioned further back from the nose than the intakes of the F-102A) and at this stage provided 15,000lb-ft of thrust or 23,500lb-ft with afterburner. The fin and rudder shape was altered entirely – with a clipped tip and swept trailing edge being the most visible differences – and some early F-106s had an extra fuel tank built into their fin. However, this feature was subsequently deleted because it could play havoc with the aircraft's centre of gravity if it failed to operate correctly.

A new undercarriage included a twin rather than single nosewheel and the cockpit was different too, drawing on experience with the F-102A. Different instruments were required for the MA-1 system and early F-106As had both centre and sidestick control columns. A key feature of the MA-1 was the Tactical

F-106A-CO DELTA DART (57-0243)

San Francisco Air Defence Sector, 456th Fighter-Interceptor Squadron, 1966. During the F-106's early years in service it was common to see the so-called 'buzz number' on the aft fuselage, as is the case with this aircraft from 456th FIS. Like so many other Delta Darts, this aircraft served with a number of different squadrons until it was send to storage at AMARC on April 1, 1985. It was pulled out of storage on March 23, 1990 and converted to a QF-106A drone. It fell victim to a AIM-7M missile exactly three years later to the day.

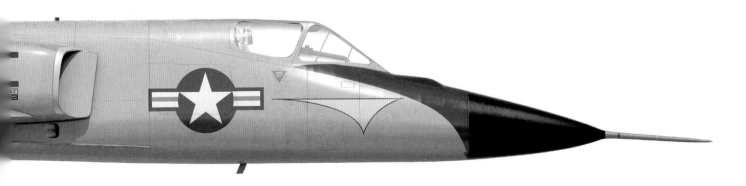

F-106A-100-CO DELTA DART (58-0787) ▽

24th Air Division, 71st Fighter-Interceptor Squadron 'Ironmen', 1970. This is among the most famous Delta Darts due to an incident that happened on February 2, 1970. While on a training mission from Malmstrom AFB the aircraft entered a flat spin which prompted Lt Gary Foust to eject. The sudden change in weight distribution caused by the pilot exiting and the ejection seat rockets firing caused the aircraft to stabilize. It flew on and eventually made a soft belly landing on a snow covered field near Big Sandy, Montana. This gave rise to the aircraft's nickname: the Cornfield Bomber. The landing was so gentle that the aircraft was eventually repaired and re-entered service in early 1972. Today the aircraft is on display at the National Museum of the United States Air Force at Wright-Patterson AFB.

F-106A-85-CO DELTA DART (57-2485) ▽

20th Air Division, 95th Fighter-Interceptor Squadron, 1970. This aircraft would be retired on June 22, 1987, and converted to a QF-106A starting on March 31, 1992. Unlike most other drones, however, this aircraft was not shot down as it suffered a mishap on April 26, 1993 – a wing spar broke, rendering it flyable. Even so, it still ended up at the bottom of the Mexican Gulf like so many other QF-106s when it was dumped there on September 25, 1995, for the purpose of creating an artificial reef.

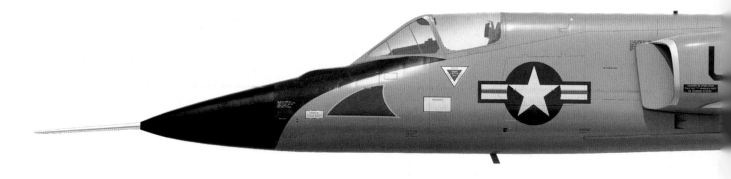

Situation Display, which allowed the pilot to visualise the mission as it unfolded through a map display projected onto the cockpit screen. The MA-1 was pre-programmed but controllers could also update it mid-flight with signals from the ground – a highly advanced feature for 1950s technology.

The F-106A was regarded as a 'weapons system', WS-201A, and as such the MA-1 was designed specifically to work with Hughes AIM-4 Falcon missiles. These would be carried internally within a fuselage weapons bay,

together with a single Douglas MB-1 unguided nuclear rocket.

The second F-106A aerodynamics testbed made its flight debut on February 26, 1957. In keeping with the new 'weapons system' approach, the F-106A was to follow a tough new testing regimen, divided into six distinct phases. Phase I was simply getting the aircraft airborne and airworthy – a process expected to be conducted by the manufacturer. Phase II was flight evaluation and this would be carried out by the Air Force.

Accordingly, the two initial prototypes were transferred to Edwards AFB and took part in performance, stability and handling trials between May 22 and June 29, 1957. These revealed several issues which Convair then had to resolve; in particular the test pilots stated that the ejection seat was completely inadequate. Designed by the Weber Aircraft Corporation, it did not have 'zero-zero' capability and needed both speed and altitude to function correctly. However, it was similarly

unable to perform if speed and altitude were too great. The other main issue identified with the F-106A was a lack of performance – Mach 1.8 being the top speed when Mach 2.0 had been expected – and a ceiling of 53,000ft, which was 7000ft lower than expected. Eighteen further recommendations were also made for improvements ranging from new pedals to canopy alternations.

None of these issues was seen as severe, since the ejection seat could be replaced and the aircraft's

performance shortfall was resolved through alterations to the aircraft's intake cowling and charging injectors. Therefore, testing moved on to Phase III which involved flame-out, spin and stall studies. It was around this time, in mid-1957, that the name Delta Dart was applied to the F-106. The first dozen F-106As to follow the prototypes off the production line all then entered the testing programme. All 12 were fitted with the J75-P-9 engine but unfortunately this was found to suffer from reliability issues and eventually all

F-106As would be fitted with the much improved and more powerful J75-P-17.

As this lengthy (for the time) process continued, the prototype F-106B two-seater made its fight flight on April 9, 1958. It had been thought that the F-106B, with its fuselage extended to house a second cockpit in tandem to the first, would be slower than the F-106A – but testing revealed that its performance matched that of the single seater. This was because the fuselage extension actually improved the airframe's aerodynamics.

Convair F-106 Delta Dart

F-106A-25-CO DELTA DART (59-0089) ▼

34th Air Division, 87th Fighter-Interceptor Squadron 'Red Bulls', 1972. 'Lurch IV' had unique nose art but unfortunately this great looking aircraft would not survive long. On November 26, 1972, it flew into a ridge shortly after take-off. The pilot did not manage to eject until it was too late and was killed in the ensuing crash.

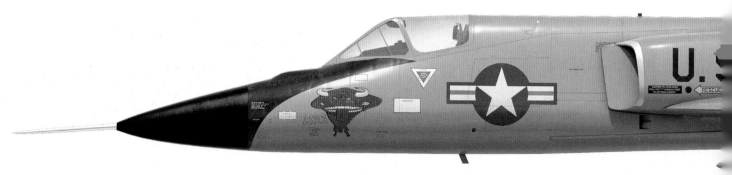

▼ F-106A-120-CO DELTA DART (59-0060)

26th Air Division, 84th Fighter-Interceptor Squadron 'Black Panthers', 1972.
This Delta Dart would serve with a number of Squadrons before ending up
as a B-1B chase plane on June 22, 1987. In August 1991 the aircraft was
converted to a QF-106 Drone. It was then shot down by an AIM-120 missile
on June 16, 1996.

▼ F-106A-CO DELTA DART (57-0241)

20th Air Division, 48th Fighter-Interceptor Squadron 'Tazlanglian Devils', 1972.
48th FIS aircraft are easily recognisable by their white trimmed tail flash. This
F-106A was put in storage at AMARC on August 8, 1985. And like many other
F-106s it was converted to QF-106 drone standard beginning on April 6,
1993. 57-0241 would fall victim to a AIM-120 missile on May 8, 1996.

Convair F-106 Delta Dart

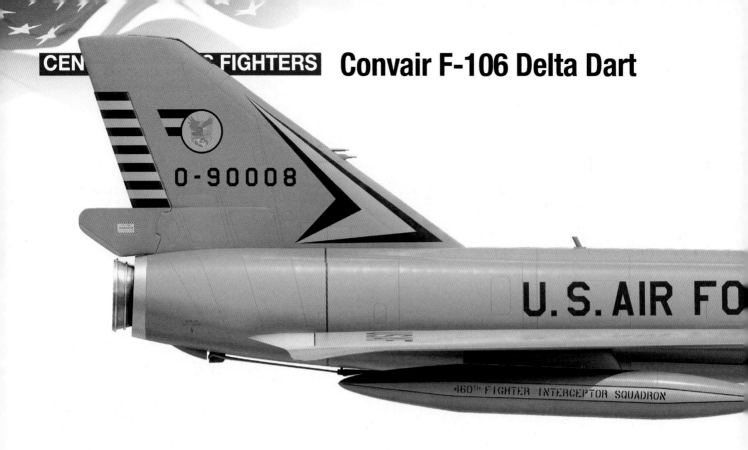

O-90008

U.S. AIR FO

460ᵀᴴ FIGHTER INTERCEPTOR SQUADRON

F-106A-CO DELTA DART (56-0459) ▼

325ᵗʰ Fighter Wing, 318ᵗʰ Fighter-Interceptor Squadron, 1976. This aircraft had a very unusual history, being assigned to Project Firewall in 1959. The goal was to break the absolute speed record and in order to make it as fast as possible the aircraft underwent a number of modifications. However, this resulted in the aircraft's engine becoming prone to compressor stalls and proved unfit for the purpose. A stock F-106A was therefore used instead (see the note on 56-0467). After the record attempt 56-0459 was taken back to standard configuration and entered squadron service. When 56-0459 was pulled from service in 1983 it was displayed at McChord Air Museum, where it still resides to this day.

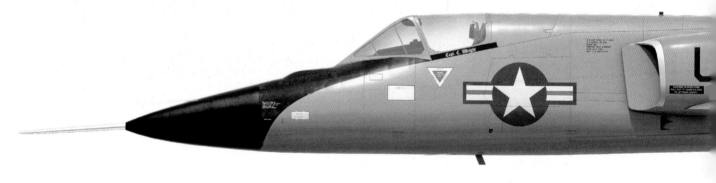

The first USAF unit to receive the F-106 was the 539th Fighter-Interceptor Squadron, on May 30, 1959, with a second unit, the 498th FIS, receiving its first example on June 1. There had originally been a plan to purchase 1000 F-106As, equipping a total of 40 squadrons. But by 1957, with advances in guided missile technology and with various other powerful aircraft types having become available or having at least entered development in the meantime, the order was cut back to just 260 F-106As, excluding the

17 examples from the initial F-106B order. As a result, the test aircraft were brought up to full production model specification and handed over for front line service.

With the F-106A's performance shortcomings addressed by 1959, when Russian test pilot Colonel Georgi Mosolov achieved a new world air speed record flying a Mikoyan-Gurevich Ye-6/3 (MiG-21) at 1484mph on October 31 that year the US was able to promptly respond with what was dubbed Project Firewall. On December 15, 1959, Major Joe W

Rogers reclaimed the title for America at the controls of a standard F-106A – hitting Mach 2.36.

In regular service use, a whole host of additional problems were discovered with the F-106, particularly with its fuel delivery system. One F-106A's canopy was accidentally jettisoned in flight during December 1959 which resulted in the whole fleet being grounded while the issue was investigated and resolved. Another source of problems was the MA-1. While it could provide remarkable capabilities when it functioned correctly, often it failed to do

▼ F-106A-105-CO DELTA DART (59-0008)

25th Air Division, 460th Fighter-Interceptor Squadron, 1973. Like many other Delta Darts this aircraft ended up as a QF-106. It was shot down by an AIM-120 missile on November 5, 1996.

so. Despite being highly advanced for its time, it was still a 1950s 'computer' and was frequently affected by glitches. During its service life, the MA-1 would receive no fewer than 60 upgrades.

During the course of 1960, all F-106As built up to that point were retrofitted with electronic countermeasures equipment as well as an anti-chaff system. While the sixth and final 'phase' of the original testing programme had concluded in 1958, in practice testing continued into 1961 – with additional problems continuing to appear and additional attempts being made to resolve them. At any one time, the USAF

had dozens of F-106s at different stages of retrofitting and modification, which made maintenance a headache. Finally, during September 1960, a programme known as Wild Goose was launched to ensure that every F-106 airframe had been brought up to the same standard.

The last F-106A was delivered on July 20, 1961, making 277 all together. Sixty-three F-106Bs had also been constructed by this point for a grand total of 340 F-106s. Just over two months later, in September 1961, the entire F-106 fleet was grounded again as fuel system problems resulted in two

crashes and the death of a pilot. Yet more modifications followed and the F-106s were cleared for flight once again. The ejection seat problems previously identified persisted however.

Even as this was happening, a potential opportunity to recommence F-106 production arose. A budget had been set aside to construct another 80 aircraft for Air Defense Command, although this was subsequently reduced to 36 by the Secretary of Defense, Robert S McNamara. Yet the USAF was reluctant to purchase more F-106s when the US Navy's promising new F4H-1

Convair F-106 Delta Dart

F-106B-80-CO DELTA DART (59-0165) ▽

Air Defense Weapons Center, 1976. This aircraft was assigned to the famous General Daniel 'Chappie' James Jr. who, at the time, was the commander of NORAD. It was destroyed in a ground fire on February 27, 1980.

F-106A-CO DELTA DART (56-0461) ▽

24th Air Division, 5th Fighter-Interceptor Squadron 'Spittin' Kittins', 1981. Unlike many other Delta Darts this aircraft was never converted into a drone. It entered storage at AMARC on April 2, 1985, and was eventually recovered on March 17, 2005, for restoration to display condition. It is now on display at KI Sawyer Heritage Air Museum where it's painted as 57-0231.

F-106A-95-CO DELTA DART (58-0764) ▽

24th Air Division, 49th Fighter-Interceptor Squadron 'Cavaliers', 1986. The 49th FIS was the last non-ANG squadron to operate the F-106 when it retired the Six on July 9, 1987. 58-0764 was among the last aircraft to leave the squadron when it was sent to AMARC on July 2, 1987. It was converted to a QF-106A drone and shot down on September 19, 1994, by an AIM-120 missile.

S. AIR FORCE

90165

AIR DEFENCE WEAPONS CENTER

.AIR FORCE

60461

★★★ 5TH FIS ★★★

AIR FORCE

80764

49TH FIS

Convair F-106 Delta Dart

0-80772

U.S. AIR FO

six pack

F-106A-95-CO DELTA DART (58-0760) ▼

125th Fighter-Interceptor Group, 159th Fighter-Interceptor Squadron 'Boxin' Gators', Florida ANG, 1976. The aircraft was painted in these colourful markings during the United States bicentennial celebrations in 1976. The end to this aircraft's existence was much less glamorous. It was converted to QF-106A standard and shot down by an AIM-7M Sparrow missile on March 2, 1993.

CI

Phantom II two-seater was being offered in an Air Force interceptor specification by McDonnell.

A 'fly-off' competition was arranged between the two types and while the Phantom's APQ-72 radar system proved both more reliable and capable than the Delta Dart's MA-1, the F-106 was said to have been more successful during visual range combat. The contest ended on November 17, 1961, but although the USAF ordered the F4H as the F-110 (to be known in service as the F-4) for Tactical Air Command, neither the F4H nor the F-106 was successful in winning

an order for ADC. The latter would have to make do with its existing F-106s.

From 1961 to 1962, another programme was commenced to retrofit and modify the F-106 fleet, known as Dart Board. This resolved the fuel problems suffered by the aircraft once and for all and a new ejection seat was installed at the same time. Known as the Convair 'B-seat', this complex design required the pilot to pull a D-ring to jettison the canopy, while at the same time his shoulder hardness was retracted and locked, as were his feet. Leg guards, seat pan and foot

pans were all raised and a second pull of the D-ring then fired the seat up on its rail before rotational thrusters pushed the seat into a horizontal position on top of the aircraft. Two long stabilisation booms then extended, attachment bolts were fired and finally a rocket motor pushed the fully reclined seat directly upwards and away from the aircraft.

Pilots disliked the new seat and eventually, in 1965, the USAF commissioned the Weber Aircraft Corporation to design a new 'zero-zero' seat for the F-106, which the

F-106A-100-CO DELTA DART (58-0772)

191st Fighter-Interceptor Group, 171st Fighter-Interceptor Squadron 'Six Pack', Michigan ANG, 1975. This aircraft entered service in September 1959 and after serving with a number of different units was eventually sent to AMARC on September 3, 1985. It would be taken out of storage in 1990 and converted to QF-106 Drone standard, eventually being shot down using an AIM-7M on September 26, 1991.

company did within just 45 days. It proved to be a success and was retrofitted to the whole F-106 fleet.

One surprising aspect of the F-106A's design was relatively good manoeuvrability at a time when an increasing reliance on missiles made this attribute seem less important. As a result, during the Vietnam War some consideration was given to sending F-106s over to provide top cover for B-52 bombing missions. Had this option been taken up, it would have been necessary to provide the aircraft with an internal cannon, a gunsight and a clearer cockpit canopy.

Although the F-106A never went to Southeast Asia, the idea of a cannon-armed variant did not go away. It was thought that the addition of a gun might aid the F-106 in its primary mission of bringing down enemy bombers and as such some effort went into working out how one could be installed. This was done under a programme known as Project Six Shooter. Eventually, it was determined that an M61A1 Vulcan with 650 rounds could be installed at the back of the weapons bay, where the MB-1 Genie would otherwise have sat. This would

allow the four AIM-4 Falcons to remain in their original positions.

The gun was to be installed in a package complete with an aerodynamic fairing to cover the cannon barrels in their position below the aircraft's fuselage. This was done and the first test firing took place on February 10, 1969. Another late 60s innovation was a pair of new underwing fuel tanks with a 360 US gallon capacity each. Going forward, these would nearly always be carried by F-106s in flight. Inflight refuelling capability was also retrofitted to surviving F-106s around this time.

F-106B-55-CO DELTA DART (57-2535) ▼

144th Fighter-Interceptor Wing, 194th Fighter-Interceptor Squadron, California ANG, 1976. Perhaps one of the most easily recognisable and unusual paint schemes ever to be worn by an F-106 was that of the California ANG during the mid-70s. Most squadrons had both single seat F-106As and twin-seat F-106Bs in their inventory, with the Bs being just as combat capable as the As. Like the As though, many Bs ended up as drones and this one is no exception. It was shot down on September 1, 1993, by an AIM-9M Sidewinder.

F-106A-95-CO DELTA DART (57-2503) ▼

102nd Fighter-Interceptor Wing, 101st Fighter-Interceptor Squadron, 1983. This aircraft survived a serious mishap when the nosegear failed to deploy while landing on December 19, 1966. It was repaired and continued in service until December 29, 1987 when it was sent to AMARC. It would later be converted into a QF-106 drone, and was shot down by an AIM-120 on April 2, 1997.

▼ F-106A-130-CO DELTA DART (59-0133)

177th Fighter-Interceptor Group, 119th Fighter-Interceptor Squadron 'Jersey Devils', New Jersey ANG, 1983. The 119th FIS was the last ANG unit to operate the F-106A, retiring it on August 1, 1988. This particular aircraft was send to AMARC on November 5, 1984, where it would remain until 1993 when it was converted to QF-106A standard. The aircraft would suffer a mishap on March 8, 1994, when the gear collapsed during landing on a manned flight. The pilot ejected and survived but the aircraft burned and was written off.

Convair F-106 Delta Dart

On May 13, 1969, a pair of F-106s stationed at Loring Air Force Base, Maine, on the extreme north-eastern tip of the United States, made the first interception of a Soviet bomber by a fighter launched from the continental United States – intercepting three Tupolev Tu-95s following a lengthy pursuit.

As the USAF's 'ultimate interceptors', F-106 units were usually stationed in the continental United States but deployments were also made to Canada, Alaska, Iceland and occasionally to Germany and South Korea. It never saw combat, however. Starting in 1972, the ADC gradually phased the type out in favour of the F-15. Surviving F-106s were then passed along to the ANG, the first to receive it being the 186th Fighter-

F-106A-95-CO DELTA DART (58-0786) ▼

125th Fighter-Interceptor Group, 159th Fighter-Interceptor Squadron 'Boxin' Gators', Florida ANG, 1984. Like so many other F-106s this aircraft was converted into a QF-106A drone. However, after surviving nine unmanned missions, it was never operated again. On April 7, 2000, it was picked up from Tyndall AFB and transported to El Paso, TX, by a private owner. It is currently stored in the desert awaiting restoration for future exhibition at the California Science Museum.

Interceptor Squadron of the Montana ANG, based at Great Falls, on April 3, 1972.

More than 16 years later, on August 1, 1988, the last official USAF F-106 flight took place when three aircraft from the 119th FIS took off from Atlantic City. Two years earlier, Flight Systems Inc. had begun taking F-106s out of long-term storage and converting them into QF-106A drones under a programme known as Pacer Six. After the first 10, another 184 were converted by the USAF itself. The last of these was shot down on February

20, 1997, with the QF-106s being replaced by QF-4 Phantom drones – which were themselves replaced with QF-16 Fighting Falcon drones starting in 2014.

The beginning of Pacer Six was not quite the end for the F-106 however. During 1997, a surviving QF-106 was used as part of a joint USAF/NASA programme known as Project Eclipse to help determine whether a large aircraft could be used to tow a vehicle carrying a payload intended for orbit up to high altitude. QF-106 59-130 was towed aloft

behind a Lockheed NC-141A Starlifter on December 20, 1997, to study whether a vehicle known as the Astroliner could be effectively towed aloft behind a Boeing 747. The idea was that the Astroliner, a rocket-propelled vehicle, would be taken to 45,000ft before its engines were ignited and it was flown up to orbit.

The last test flight of this QF-106 was on February 6, 1998, and the last flight of any F-106 was when the same aircraft was flown from Edwards AFB, where Project Eclipse had been based, to AMARC.

▼ **F-106A-75-CO DELTA DART (57-2463)**

120th Fighter-Interceptor Group, 186th Fighter-Interceptor Squadron, Montana ANG, 1984. After being converted to a QF-106A this aircraft crash landed on its seventh mission (May 9, 1994) and was written off.

Convair F-106 Delta Dart

F-106B-31-CO DELTA DART (57-2516) ▼

Assigned to NASA, 1982. Several F-106 were assigned to NASA for different purposes. This aircraft was used to investigate the effects of lightning strikes on aircraft. It was deliberately flown into thunderstorms and struck by lightning and thereby gathered vital information for use on military and commercial aircraft. One of the effects of the lightning was the paint peeling off, creating an unusual pattern of weathering. The aircraft was retired on May 17, 1991, and put on display at the Virginia Air and Space Center in Hampton, Virginia.

F-106B-31-CO DELTA DART (57-2513)

B-1B chase aircraft, 1986. Several F-106s (both A and B models) were used as chase aircraft for the B-1B Lancer test flights during the 1980s. The aircraft entered storage at AMARC on June 25, 1990, only to re-enter service on November 2, 1990, with the 425th Weapons Evaluation Group at Tyndall AFB in support of the QF-106 drone programme.

QF-106Q-70-CO DELTA DART (57-2459)

6585th Test Group, 1992. The QF-106 drones operated out of Tyndall AFB were typically shot down over the Caribbean Sea. Many retained some evidence of their former squadron affiliation and this one is no exception. The blue triangles on the rudder and the arrow on the droptank indicate that this aircraft was flying with the 186th FIS before it was retired and converted. Unusually, this aircraft wasn't shot down – being salvaged for spare parts instead on June 4, 1996.

NORTH AMERICAN F-107A 'ULTRA SABRE'

What became the F-107A started out as an all-weather fighter-bomber version of the F-100A – the F-100B. Extensive development work saw the design radically changed and the result was a competitor for the F-105. Three prototypes were built but the type never entered full series production.

With the F-100A originally envisioned as a pure fighter, the designation F-100B was given to North American designs NA-211/NA-212 – which would be an all-weather fighter-bomber companion for the 'A'. The company commenced work on NA-212 in 1953 just as the YF-100s were being tested and the first F-100As were rolling off the production line.

However, the USAF quickly decided that the F-100A itself should be given fighter-bomber capability – so North American concentrated on adapting the basic F-100 design to this purpose and NA-211/NA-212 instead became the basis for a possible F-100 successor. The new aircraft would be a tactical fighter capable of carrying nuclear munitions to speeds above Mach 2 and operating from rough landing sites. While the earliest drafts showed an aircraft very similar to the F-100A but with a longer nose, later drawings of the NA-211 saw the familiar oval nose intake replaced with an underslung V-type intake.

The alternative layout, NA-212, featured the same V-type intake but positioned on top of the fuselage instead and it was this design which attracted the USAF's interest. Shifting the intake to this position prevented any aerodynamic interference with a nuclear payload carried beneath the aircraft and also significantly reduced the possibility of foreign objects being ingested if the aircraft had to operate from a makeshift airfield.

Nine aircraft were ordered as the F-107 (giving the type a firm spot within the 'Century Series') but this was eventually curtailed to just three F-107A prototypes. Informally, the design was known as the 'Ultra Sabre'.

Although the design was intended to eventually fly above Mach 2, each prototype was to be powered by a single Pratt & Whitney YJ75-P-11 afterburning turbojet with 17,200lb-ft of thrust (24,500lb with afterburner) – providing a top speed of 890mph (Mach 1.15) at sea level or 1295mph (Mach 1.69) at 36,000ft. From its wings back towards its tail, the aircraft resembled the F-100 on which it was based, though the wings were of thinner chord and an 'all-moving' tailfin was fitted. There was an under-fuselage recess where a nuclear bomb or a drop tank could be carried and armament was to consist of four cannon.

The forward part of the aircraft, however, bore no resemblance to the F-100 – with the all-new intake design featuring prominently. There were big changes within the cockpit too, an early fly-by-wire system being installed.

The first flight of F-107A-NA 55-5118, with North American test pilot Joel Robert 'Bob' Baker at the controls, took place at Edwards Air Force Base on September 10, 1956. Baker reached a speed of Mach 1.03 but when he came in to land the drogue parachute failed to deploy and as the aircraft sped down the runway the nosewheel strut collapsed, causing minor damage.

The second prototype, 55-5119, was fitted with four 20mm M39 cannon and used for weapons testing. The third, 55-5120, was used to test a continuously variable engine intake design.

The F-107A was defeated by Republic's F-105 (though the F-105 itself was nearly cancelled on several occasions, as previously related). As a result, two of the three F-107As were turned over to NASA's predecessor, NACA, for flight research purposes. 55-5118 made just four flights for NACA before being grounded, while 55-5120 managed 42. The former survives today at the Pima Air and Space Museum in Arizona while the latter was damaged on take-off on September 1, 1959. It ended up in poor condition at the Tallmantz Museum in California during the 1960s before being scrapped. 55-5119 also survives – at the National Museum of the USAF at Wright-Patterson AFB, Ohio.

1956–1959

F-107A-NA 'ULTRA SABRE' (55-5118)

The first prototype of the F-107A went supersonic during its first flight on September 10, 1956. The aircraft was extensively used for tests and would eventually be loaned to NACA at Dryden for high-speed testing. When the F-107 programme was cancelled, the aircraft was put on display. Today it can be seen at the Pima Air and Space Museum.

U.S. AIR FORCE

55118

F107A

NORTH AMERICAN XF-108 'RAPIER'

Designed to address problems inherent in the XF-103's design, North American's unbuilt XF-108 was the last in a line of 1950s advanced interceptor programmes.

1955-1959

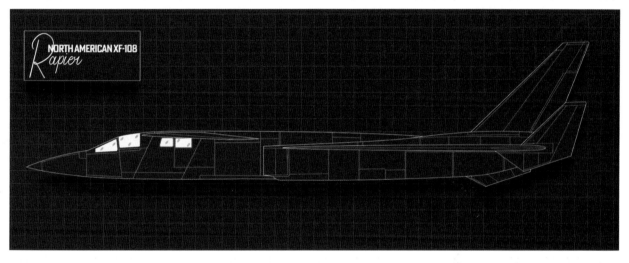

NORTH AMERICAN XF-108
Rapier

Supremely overconfident in its own abilities, Republic had bitten off more than it could chew with the XF-103 interceptor design. Working with titanium proved to be a nightmare and the whole concept was fundamentally flawed.

The XF-103 had room for only the pilot – who would have to manage everything from communications and navigation to the aircraft's radar and weapons systems in addition to actually flying the aircraft. And doing the latter effectively would be difficult given the severely restricted visibility available from the submerged cockpit.

In addition, the aircraft's slender fuselage, despite being physically huge, could house only one turbojet and offered precious little room for fuel and payload. Range was short, weaponry was limited and the airframe had absolutely no potential for development or adaptability for other roles.

The USAF eventually came to understand these inherent limitations and therefore devised a new requirement for a Long-Range Interceptor – Experimental (LRIX), which was issued as GOR 114 on October 6, 1955. This called for a more flexible and capable twin-engine interceptor with a capacious fuselage and a crew of two. The necessary performance

would still be Mach 3+ but it was believed that this could now be achieved with conventional turbojets rather than having to rely on a ramjet that would need years of additional development time.

Designs for GOR 114 were tendered by Lockheed, North American and Northrop in early 1956, with North American design NA-236 being chosen for development. After 18 months, the latest version of the design, NA-257, was given the designation XF-108 and a contract for two prototypes was awarded to the company on June 6, 1957.

The XF-108 would be a large delta-winged aircraft with a single central fin, powered by two General Electric J93-GE-3AR turbojets. The crew would be seated in tandem, each in their own ejection capsule, and the aircraft would feature cutting-edge avionics with a Hughes-designed AN/ASG-18 radar. Armament would be three of the latest Hughes Falcon missiles in an internal weapons bay.

A mock-up of the XF-108 was inspected in January 1959 and the programme was officially given the name 'Rapier' four months later, on May 15, 1959. At this stage it was calculated that the XF-108 would be able to reach Mach 2.58 at an altitude of 75,550ft and would have an operational radius of 1020 miles.

Technologically, North American was on track with the XF-108 by mid-1959. General Electric was also on track with the J93 – which was also specified for the company's Mach 3+ bomber, the XB-70 Valkyrie.

However, after a decade of working on high-performance interceptors to tackle the threat of Soviet nuclear bombers it was becoming clear that the Soviets had switched their attention to ballistic nuclear missiles instead. While the bomber threat remained, it was unlikely that wave after wave of them would appear over the continental United States. It was far more likely that the Soviets would launch waves of missiles instead – which no piloted interceptor would be able to shoot down.

Similarly, North American's XB-70 became increasingly pointless when the US itself was building up its own stockpile of long-range ballistic nuclear missiles. As a result, both the Rapier and the Valkyrie programmes were halted. While work on a pair of XB-70 prototypes was allowed to continue, the XF-108 was stopped in September 1959 before any could be constructed.

The Hughes AN/ASG-18 radar survived the death of the XF-108, however, and was switched over to the YF-12A programme – which itself would ultimately be cancelled after the construction of three prototypes.

BELL 'XF-109'

Bell's D-188A supersonic VSTOL fighter design was intended to provide multirole capability for both the USAF and the US Navy but no prototype was constructed... at least not in America.

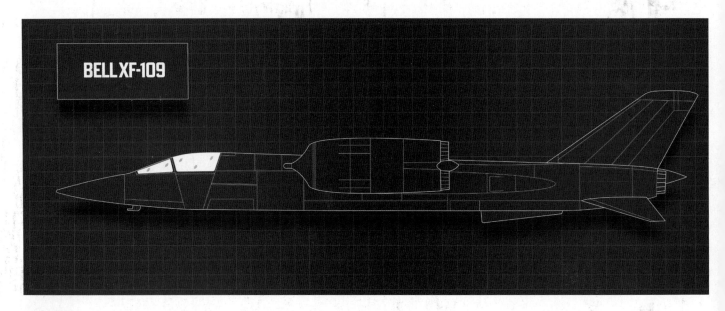

BELL XF-109

1955-1961

Throughout the early years of the cold war there was huge interest from air forces around the world in the concept of a high-performance fighter capable of taking off without a runway.

Both the USAF and the US Navy foresaw a multitude of possibilities for such an aircraft – which could be easily operated from a jungle clearing or from the deck of a small vessel out at sea. While most American aircraft manufacturers of the period worked on vertical and/or short take-off and landing fighter designs, the firm that came closest to actually getting one built was Bell.

The company drew up a design known as D-188A in 1955 and offered it to the USAF and US Navy. The aircraft was to be a long and slender single-seater with short wings and a conventional tail. Armament would be four 20mm cannon with the option to carry up to 108 FFARs and 4000lb of bombs.

Power would come from no fewer than eight General Electric J85-GE-5 turbojets, providing 2600lb-ft of thrust each. Four of these would be fitted to the aircraft's wingtips, two on each tip, in nacelles. The nacelles would be positioned vertically for take-off before rotating to a horizontal attitude for flight.

The other four jets would be housed within the aircraft's fuselage – two at the back, exhausting to the rear, and two just behind the cockpit positioned vertically to help with take-offs and landings. A maximum speed of Mach 2.3 was expected, along with a ceiling of 60,000ft and a combat radius of 1350 miles. Bell was commissioned to build a mock-up of the D-188A in 1957 and this was duly constructed. Following a positive response, the company apparently requested that its design be given the designation XF-109 in USAF service, with XF3L-1 being the preferred Navy designation.

The 'F-109' had supposedly been tentatively applied to numerous projects prior to this point – a two-seat all-weather variant of the McDonnell F-101 in 1955, the Ryan X-13 Vertijet of the same year, and what became the F-106B. However, although Bell probably came closest to receiving the number, it too joined this list of 'nearly F-109s'.

The request for the number was reportedly denied but the programme persisted for a surprisingly long time. The Navy gave up on it in 1960 but the USAF remained interested until it was finally cancelled during the spring of 1961. However, a remarkably similar-looking design was produced by a German consortium known as Entwicklungsring Süd in 1959.

Entwicklungsring Süd consisted of aircraft companies Messerschmitt, Heinkel and Bölkow and was formed for the express purpose of developing this design, known as the VJ 101, for the German air force. The VJ 101 was powered by six Rolls-Royce/MAN RB.145 turbojets – two in each swivelling wingtip nacelle and two in the fuselage behind the cockpit to help with take-offs and landings.

The aircraft was intended to be a Mach 2 VSTOL interceptor and two prototypes were built and flown successfully during the mid-1960s, with the programme only being cancelled in 1968. Exactly how much the German design owed to Bell's earlier project is unclear but the VJ 101 certainly demonstrated the validity of the concept even if it ultimately lost out to the Hawker-Siddeley Harrier.